TABLE OF CONTENTS:

Introduction to Fabulous Recipes for Vibrant Health	Page 2
Breakfast (including smoothies and juicing ideas)	Page 5
Healthy Snacks and Appetizers	Page 29
Heart Warming Soups and Stews	Page 46
Sumptuous Salads and Vegetable Side Dishes	Page 84
Pasta and Pasta Alternatives	Page 113
Whole Grain Comforts and Hearty Main Dishes	Page 128
Truly Healthy and Decadent Desserts	Page 145

Visit *www.sanaview.com* to get many juicy free downloadable offers to improve your life NOW!

Janet McKee Success Coach, Wellness Expert, Speaker and Author
CEO and Founder of SanaView
janet@sanaview.com
©SanaView 2018. All rights reserved.

INTRODUCTION

*Thank you for considering the recipes in this book to help inspire you to live a healthier and more vibrant life. As a Wellness Expert and long-time Holistic Health Practitioner, I have seen time and time again as clients begin to eat healthier foods, they are amazed at how much better they feel and are excited to continue to try even more great recipes and ideas. Often, someone will come to see me because they were diagnosed with a serious health challenge. As I teach them the importance of nourishing their body in the best way possible, they begin to experience a healthier more comfortable digestive system, they begin to feel greater energy and excitement for life, the look of their skin and eyes improves and their weight naturally balances to a level that is ideal for their body type. So, as they are dealing with a serious health concern, their friends and family begin to tell them that they **look** better than ever. And of course, they begin to **feel** better than ever, both physically and emotionally. It is quite amazing.*

The key here is to learn that healthy foods also taste amazingly delicious and can satisfy all cravings for various tastes and textures. When you are enjoying great tasting and fulfilling foods that also support your health and well-being, it becomes so easy to stick with this new lifestyle. Feeling deprived is no way to live. You want to feel satisfied and enjoy beautiful and delicious food. This is the key to making these positive life-affirming changes in a way that becomes easy for you to stick with the rest of your life. When you enjoy the food choices you are making and at the same time feel better than ever, why wouldn't you want to make this a lifelong choice?

I too had experienced a very serious health challenge years ago. In my twenties I was diagnosed with Ulcerative Colitis, which is a serious inflammatory bowel disease and autoimmune disorder. I was told I had to be on medication the rest of my life and that there was no hope to ever resolve the illness and heal my body. Well, as I progressed through life, my illness got progressively worse. As we increased the dosages of medications, we unfortunately concluded, after landing in the hospital with internal bleeding that wouldn't stop, that I was actually allergic to the medications available for UC. I was left with a choice to either get on one additional med that had a concerning rate of causing cancer, or have my lower intestines surgically removed. As you may guess by now, I chose neither option and I began my journey of learning how to heal my body naturally. Through several years of trial and error, I discovered that the body can heal itself, even when facing the direst consequences, and that food and emotions both play a major role. I have lived illness and medication free for over 20 years.

Janet McKee Success Coach, Wellness Expert, Speaker and Author
CEO and Founder of SanaView
janet@sanaview.com
©SanaView 2018. All rights reserved.

Food is what nourishes every cell of your body and supports your immune system. And when you realize that each thing you put in your mouth is either going to support your health and well-being or detract from it, the choice becomes very clear. You will want to support your health with each positive life-giving choice. Through the years of trial-and-error, I discovered ways to make food that is extremely healthy and extremely delicious too.

Later as I studied and became a certified holistic health practitioner, I had many clients ask me for recipe ideas to support what I was teaching them about how food supports the body. So, through the years I compiled a set of simple recipes that my clients loved. Many, as you may imagine, asked me to put all of my recommended recipes together in a book for them to use. These are not all of my recipes but this is a collection of most of the recipes I use when working with clients. This new edition with even more of my favorite recipes is finally here for you to explore and enjoy.

As part of my practice, I was selected to be the local representative for PCRM (Physicians Committee for Responsible Medicine) run by Dr. Neal Barnard out of Washington DC. As an instructor for PCRM, I teach how food helps to prevent cancer and diabetes and how these foods help to improve survival once diagnosed. We use in the Food For Life classes, "The Cancer Survivor's Guide", which is an amazing book filled with nutrition information and recipes to teach how food fights cancer. I have come to love several of the simple recipes from this book and use them often in teaching my classes and in working with clients. You will see a small subset of some of their recipes in this book.

Several years ago, I was asked to cater all of the food for the Mayan Elders who came to Pittsburgh. They came here to announce that the city is a sacred site because of the 3 rivers coming together to a point with a fourth underground river (which feeds the fountain at the point). So, I had to do some research as to what foods Mayan's enjoyed. I had created a small Mayan cookbook that held all the recipes we used during the weeklong catering event. Some of those recipes are included in this book and are noted with a reference to the Mayan collection.

And finally, you may see a few things that seem unfamiliar such as some exotic ingredients, like young coconuts or raw cacao powder, and some reference to raw foods. Please don't be thrown off by these ideas and ingredients. Feel free to contact me with any questions and I will be glad to assist.

Janet McKee Success Coach, Wellness Expert, Speaker and Author

CEO and Founder of SanaView

janet@sanaview.com

©SanaView 2018. All rights reserved.

During my years of trial and error in learning how to heal my body, I came across the raw food nutritional theory to healing the body. The concept here is that by eating fresh fruits, vegetables, nuts and seeds, you are able to access the natural enzymes that are available in these foods in an uncooked state. Within the raw food practice, many like to dehydrate, which only heats the foods at low temperatures. This gives the foods more of a cooked taste and texture without killing the enzymes. You will see some recipes that refer to dehydrating. If you don't have a dehydrator, then putting them in the oven at low temperatures may work as well.

Bringing in fresh fruits and vegetables into my diet actually did lead me to the final phase of my healing. I greatly enjoy the health benefits of including fresh uncooked ingredients into my daily meals. Please do consider incorporating 70 - 80% raw foods into your diet for healing and rejuvenation.

Thank you again for exploring ways to improve your health deliciously. Good food and good health support a happy and healthy life, and that is my wish for you.
Peace and blessings
Janet

Janet McKee Success Coach, Wellness Expert, Speaker and Author
CEO and Founder of SanaView
janet@sanaview.com
©SanaView 2018. All rights reserved.

BREAKFAST

Breakfast is such an amazing meal. When you start your day with something delicious and satisfying that is extremely good for you too, you are certainly starting your day in a healthy, balanced and energizing way. It is so easy, too, to start the day with incredibly delicious healthy foods. Fruit, which is often a part of a wonderful morning meal, along with nuts or whole grains can all make your first meal of the day enjoyable.

There are such a wide variety of colorful fruits available, that there is no reason to get bored with the same old thing every day. They are sweet and delicious, naturally hydrating and provide the fiber, nutrients, antioxidants, and healthy carbs your body needs to begin the day. They also support a healthy digestive system, which is critical to getting your day off on the right foot.

Enjoy fruits, either fresh or frozen, in smoothies, fresh juices, with nuts and seeds to provide healthy fats and protein to start you day and balance your blood sugar. Putting fruit and nuts over a bowl of steel cut oats or brown rice or quinoa porridge is wonderful too. Many love grains for breakfast, which can be wonderful for the body. I recommend true whole grains such as steel cut oatmeal or even the wonderful gluten free grains such as brown rice, quinoa, millet or buckwheat. These can be eaten alone or combined into a wonderful breakfast porridge. Of course I always recommend adding some fruit and nuts and cinnamon to the bowl of grains to round out the meal.

One of my favorite breakfast ideas is a simple bowl of chopped fruit that is in season topped with raw almond or walnut butter and/or crushed nuts and seeds. Or, I combine many wonderful ingredients into any of an assortment of smoothie ideas. None of these options take long to prepare so I can eat and run quickly while knowing that I nourished my body in the best way possible to start my day.

I also love to include green leafy vegetables in my morning meal. One way is to sauté with garlic and onions and other wonderful vegetables. This is a great alternative to the standard fried egg that many rely on for breakfast. Another interesting and delicious way to include greens is by combining this into a smoothie with fruit. This is what has been termed a "green smoothie". This not only tastes wonderful as the sweetness and flavors of the fruit hide the taste of the greens, it is also mineralizing and alkalizing for the body. And of course, a fresh juice with wheat grass and other greens

Janet McKee Success Coach, Wellness Expert, Speaker and Author
CEO and Founder of SanaView
janet@sanaview.com
©SanaView 2018. All rights reserved.

along with celery and cucumber and carrots or apples to sweeten, is an amazing way to energize your day.

Please be sure to experiment with these new ideas that you will see in the following pages and enjoy a great breakfast each day. You have fasted all night and need to boost your metabolism, body chemistry, your energy and your mood with a healthy and delicious breaking of the fast.

Janet McKee Success Coach, Wellness Expert, Speaker and Author
CEO and Founder of SanaView
janet@sanaview.com
©SanaView 2018. All rights reserved.

Smoothie Inspiration

Blending foods can be wonderful for the taste buds and easy on the digestive system at the same time. It is a good idea to blend foods to assist with digestion and assimilation of nutrients as the blender helps to begin to break down the foods. A fruit smoothie, with added protein, healthy fats, and greens makes for a nutritious breakfast or snack. You determine the amount of each ingredient so that the taste is to your liking.

For all recipes to follow, just place the ingredients in a good quality blender, blend and enjoy!

Simple Fruit Smoothies:

Select favorite fruits and combine frozen and fresh if available. Add some fresh apple, grape or pear juice with water for more flavor and sweetness. Bananas in the smoothie add sweetness and creaminess. If you desire additional sweetness, consider adding stevia, Organic Zero or Lakanto (natural no calorie sweeteners) or honey, agave or pure maple syrup.

Janet McKee Success Coach, Wellness Expert, Speaker and Author
CEO and Founder of SanaView
janet@sanaview.com
©SanaView 2018. All rights reserved.

The following are some examples to help inspire you:
- Frozen berries, apple juice and water
- Frozen berries, bananas and water
- Frozen or fresh bananas with frozen peaches or mangoes and water
- Watermelon, frozen raspberries, ginger
- Watermelon, honey (optional), cantaloupe, lime juice, o.j., mint leaf
- Banana, peach, frozen raspberries or strawberries, orange juice
- Apple juice, blueberries, strawberries, hemp seeds, pinch of sea salt, vanilla, water
- Grapes, pineapple, water

- Watermelon and raw cacao powder (or a good organic cocoa powder)
- Cantaloupe chunks and seeds and a pinch of cinnamon – this tastes like a creamsicle

Janet McKee Success Coach, Wellness Expert, Speaker and Author
CEO and Founder of SanaView
janet@sanaview.com
©SanaView 2018. All rights reserved.

Consider add-ins to any smoothie to boost nutrition:

- Bee Pollen
- Ground Flax Seeds
- Hemp Seeds
- Chia Seeds
- Aloe Vera
- Nut butters
- Green powders or Spirulina (consult Janet for wonderful recommendations)
- Healthy Plant-based Protein Powders (consult Janet for wonderful recommendations)
- Green Leafy vegetables (see Green Smoothie Inspiration on Page 8)

Non-Dairy Milk Smoothies: Consider using almond, rice, soy, hemp, oat or coconut milk or make your own by trying the nut and seed milk recipe in the following pages:

- Non-dairy milk and frozen cherries
- Non-dairy milk, cherries and raw cacao powder
- Non-dairy milk, cherries, banana, cacao powder
- Non-dairy milk, peaches and bananas

Chocolate Banana Smoothie:
- 3 cups of frozen bananas chopped
- 2 cups of non-dairy milk
- 1 tsp vanilla extract
- 2 T of cocoa, raw cacao or carob powder
- Pinch of sea salt

Blue Sunset (adapted from Raw Food Real World)
- 2 cups pineapple chunks
- 1 small ripe banana or 1 cup of frozen chopped banana
- 1 cup diced mango
- 1 ½ cups of non-dairy milk
- 2 fresh dates (optional if you need it to be sweeter)
- 2 T vanilla extract
- Pinch of sea salt
- Blend all of the above and pour half into serving glasses filling glasses ½ full.
- Add 1 cup of blueberries to what is remaining in the blender and pour on top

Berry Smoothie (from The Cancer Survivor's Guide)
- 2 – 3 cups of non-dairy milk
- 2 cups of frozen bananas
- 2 cups of either frozen strawberries or blueberries
- 4 T apple juice concentrate
- 1 tsp vanilla extract

Janet McKee Success Coach, Wellness Expert, Speaker and Author
CEO and Founder of SanaView
janet@sanaview.com
©SanaView 2018. All rights reserved.

Apple Pie Smoothie:
- 2 cups non-dairy milk
- 1 apple chopped
- ½ cup pecans
- ¼ cup coconut flakes
- 1 frozen banana
- 1 tsp vanilla
- ½ tsp cinnamon

Peach Mango Smoothie
- 2 – 3 cups of nut milk or any non-dairy milk
- 2 cups of frozen bananas
- 2 cups of either frozen peaches and mangoes or any fruit of choice
- 4 T apple juice concentrate (or ½ cup organic bottled juice)
- 1 tsp vanilla extract

Nut Milk Protein Smoothie:
- Nut milk
- vanilla extract
- 5 T hemp seeds or protein powder (consult Janet about a good protein powder)
- ½ banana
- Blueberries

Nate's Favorite Breakfast Smoothie (my son loves this in the morning!):
- 1 cup frozen blueberries
- 1 banana (fresh or frozen)
- 1 T ground flax seed
- 2 T hemp seed
- 1 cup non-dairy milk
- (we also add a handful of spinach or other greens – see green smoothie ideas below)

Janet McKee Success Coach, Wellness Expert, Speaker and Author
CEO and Founder of SanaView
janet@sanaview.com
©SanaView 2018. All rights reserved.

Other creative Smoothie Ideas:

Tropical Smoothie:
- 2 cups frozen pineapple
- 2 cups frozen mango
- 3 frozen or fresh bananas
- 4 cups of orange juice

Hemp Protein Smoothie:
- ¼ cup shelled hemp seeds
- 1 scoop of protein powder of choice (optional)
- 1 ¼ cups water
- 1 ripe banana
- 1 handful of frozen strawberries
- Cacao powder can be added as an option

Blueberry Watermelon Freeze (from American Institute for Cancer Research)
- 1 ¾ cup cubed frozen watermelon
- ¾ cup frozen blueberries
- 2 tsp chopped fresh ginger
- ¼ cup apple juice concentrate
- 1 T lime juice
- ¼ cup water
- Fresh mint for garnish

Green Smoothies:

Sneaking some greens in with your fruit is a smart choice to up your intake of greens throughout the day. With the fruit providing the main flavor, the greens are hardly noticeable. Put in the blender, half fruit of choice with half green leafy vegetable of choice along with water or additional fruit juice. Choose any greens you like with some celery to aid in digestion.

The following are some examples to help inspire you:
- Banana, blueberry, celery, green leafy vegetable of choice (such as parsley, cilantro, spinach, kale, sprouts, Swiss chard etc.)
  (Add ground flax, aloe and green powders for added nutrition)
- Banana, mango, greens, water
- Romaine lettuce, watermelon, water
- Romaine, grapes, orange, banana, water
- Mango, parsley (or any green), water
- Peaches, spinach, water
- Grapes, pineapple, greens, water
- Pears, raspberries, kale, water

Cleansing Smoothies:
- Cucumber, Cilantro, Spinach, Pineapple, Lemon, Ginger, Parsley

Or

- Pink grapefruit, cucumber, cilantro, lime, pineapple, vanilla, a pinch of sea salt and water
-

Low Glycemic Smoothie (this is excellent for diabetics or anyone avoiding sweet fruit):
- One peeled lemon
- ½ cup parsley
- 1 rib celery
- 1 – 2 cups of spinach or leafy green of choice
- A small bit of peeled ginger
- 1 cucumber
- 2 granny smith apples
- water

Janet McKee Success Coach, Wellness Expert, Speaker and Author
CEO and Founder of SanaView
janet@sanaview.com
©SanaView 2018. All rights reserved.

Superfood Smoothies:

These smoothies use some ingredients that some consider "superfoods" because of their potential powerful nutrients. These smoothies are adapted from Shanti Devi Michal, who is a raw chef from New York who performed a raw food demonstration that I attended back in 2005. I met one of my closest friends at this demo who has become a lifelong friend. The first one here is my favorite!

Blueberry Banana Protein Smoothie
- 1 cup of frozen or fresh bananas
- 1 cup of frozen wild blueberries
- 1 T spirulina
- 1 tsp maca (optional)
- ½ cup hemp seeds
- 1 – 2 T cacao nibs or powder
- ½ vanilla stick or ½ tsp vanilla extract
- Pinch of sea salt
- Squeeze of lemon
- Water from one young Thai coconut (optional)
- Fill the rest of the blender with water

Strawberry Peach Maca Smoothie
- 2 cups of frozen strawberries
- 2 cups of frozen peaches
- 1 cup of young coconut meat, cashews or pine nuts
- 1 tsp lemon juice
- 1 T maca
- 3 tsp cacao nibs or powder
- 3 drops of vanilla extract
- 2 – 4 T agave nectar (or banana or dates to sweeten)
- Pinch of salt
- Water

Smoothie Bowls – Chocolate Cherry Acai Bowl:

If you don't want to drink your breakfast, how about making your smoothie thicker and adding some crunchy nuts on top to enjoy chewing your morning smoothie! You can do this with any of the smoothie ideas above but here is my favorite chocolate, cherry, Acai combination.

Ingredients:
¼ cup hemp seeds
½ cup water
a few drops of almond extract
1 cup of frozen bananas
1 cup of frozen cherries
1 T cacao or cocoa powder
a pinch of sea salt
optional ½ package of frozen acai
optional ½ tsp ground flax and/or chia seeds
toppings of choice such as fresh berries, nuts and seeds

Preparation:
Blend the hemp seeds, water and almond extract first.
Add the frozen fruit, cacao powder and sea salt and blend.
Top with fresh berries, nuts, seeds, coconut and goji berries

Servings: 1 - 2

Nut or Seed Milk

As most of my health clients and lecture attendees know, I recommend eliminating dairy foods from the diet. Many health challenges seem to be exacerbated from consuming milk and cheese etc. Luckily, there are many non-dairy milk alternatives available in the grocery stores today. Still, homemade non-dairy milks are the most delicious and it is reassuring to know that you control the ingredients.

Ingredients:
1 cup of fresh raw almonds, Brazil nuts, cashews, hemp seeds or sesame seeds
5 cups fresh spring or filtered water (less water for thicker consistency)
Dash of sea salt
1 tsp alcohol free vanilla extract or whole vanilla bean

Preparation:
Soak the almonds in water for 8 – 12 hours or Brazil nuts and cashews for at least 15 minutes. Seeds typically do not need to be soaked. Drain and rinse the soaked nuts. Add the nuts or seeds to a blender with the water, sea salt and vanilla and blend. It is suggested that you pour the milk through a nut milk bag to remove any of the nut solids.

Servings: 5

Janet McKee Success Coach, Wellness Expert, Speaker and Author
CEO and Founder of SanaView
janet@sanaview.com
©SanaView 2018. All rights reserved.

Simple Juicing Suggestions

Drinking fresh juice is one of the most healing and cleansing things you can do for your body. Since your body is not working hard to digest, the nutrients are absorbed immediately and this offers your body's cells an opportunity to cleanse and rejuvenate.

I do recommend you use a good quality juicer and I can make specific recommendations to you and get for you dealer pricing, so feel free to contact me directly. A good juicer is very thorough and will yield the most juice from fruits and vegetables with little pulp remaining. These juicers are able to juice wheat grass and green leafy vegetables as well as fruits and more solid vegetables. A lower quality juicer is better for straight fruit juices, such as orange juice, because it is not as thorough with the pulp and the juice is more drinkable. Please contact me if you are interested in one of these juicers as I am able to offer discount pricing.

You can juice just about any fruit and vegetable. If you have an overabundance of something from your garden in the summer, don't hesitate to throw it in the juicer.

Janet McKee Success Coach, Wellness Expert, Speaker and Author
CEO and Founder of SanaView
janet@sanaview.com
©SanaView 2018. All rights reserved.

Begin light with just:
- Apple
- Celery

Then consider adding any of the following:
- Romaine, parsley or cilantro
- Kale, collards, dandelion, spinach or any green you have on hand
  (*Be sure to consider beet and carrot tops as they are highly nutritious* greens)
- Beets
- Carrots
- Cucumber
- Lemons or Oranges or Limes
- Cabbage
- Ginger
- Burdock Root
- Broccoli (or just the stems you removed and typically discard)
- Pears
- Grapes (with the seeds if you can find them)
- Pomegranates
- Fresh Cranberries
- Sweet red peppers
- Wheat Grass
- Sprouts

The following are some examples to help inspire you:
Parsley, apple, and celery
Apple, celery, and lemon
Apple, celery, and burdock root
Apple, celery, and cucumber
Apple, peach, cucumber, green pepper, red pepper, parsley
Carrot, cucumber, sprouts, greens, and lemon
Cucumber, celery, lemon, ginger, kale, and apple
Kale, dandelion, spinach, cucumber, burdock root, celery, apple, lemon or orange
Kale, cucumber, celery, spinach, parsley, collards, lemon, and apple
Kale, celery, apple, lemon, carrot, cucumber, fresh ginger and possibly turmeric root
Carrot, beet, Swiss chard, parsley, apple and lemon
Wheat grass, spinach, celery, carrots or beets, and apple

Janet McKee Success Coach, Wellness Expert, Speaker and Author
CEO and Founder of SanaView
janet@sanaview.com
©SanaView 2018. All rights reserved.

Raw Nut-Based Breakfast Porridge

It is wonderful sometimes to enjoy a creamy and delicious breakfast without grains for a change of pace. This recipe is a truly yummy one that I learned from a friend in NY.

Ingredients:
3 cups of almonds or Brazil nuts soaked
    Note: almonds should be soaked at least 8 hours, Brazil nuts at least 15 minutes
1 apple cored and chopped
1 T cinnamon
1 small piece of fresh ginger (optional)
1 tsp sea salt

Nut milk – see recipe on page 16

Preparation:
Drain and rinse the nuts after soaking.
Process all of the ingredients in a blender with enough nut milk until smooth and creamy.

Add additional chopped apples, raisins or fresh berries or your fruit of choice.
Pour nut milk over and serve.

Servings: 4

Warm Grain Porridge from Janet's book, "Mayan Inspired Recipes"

Grains, such as quinoa, have been widely used throughout central and south America. The grains are high in protein and like millet, are gluten free. You can use just one grain or combine grains together for interest and appeal. Be sure to soak and drain the millet and quinoa before cooking to clean the grains, reduce phytic acid and reduce bitterness.

Ingredients:
1 cup each of two grains of choice such as quinoa, millet, or steel cut oats
4 cups water
A handful of raisins or currants
Optional garnishes:
Chopped apples, berries, bananas, walnuts, almonds, dried coconut, cinnamon, and non-dairy milk such as almond or coconut milk

Preparation:
Combine 4 cups of water and 2 cups of grain in a small pot or saucepan and bring to a boil.
Turn temperature down and simmer until grains are tender.
When combining grains, cook as long as the longest cooking grain (quinoa 15 mins, millet and oats 30 mins).
Add a handful of raisins or currants while cooking to add sweetness and flavor.

When the grains are done, spoon into a bowl and add milk, nuts, fruit and cinnamon as desired.

Servings: 6 - 8

Janet McKee Success Coach, Wellness Expert, Speaker and Author
CEO and Founder of SanaView
janet@sanaview.com
©SanaView 2018. All rights reserved.

Sautéed Veggies and Potatoes

For my clients who love fried eggs in the morning but who are trying to lower their cholesterol or improve their health overall, I love to suggest this delicious savory breakfast alternative that is so good, you may enjoy it for lunch or dinner too.

Ingredients:
1 T olive oil or coconut oil
1-2 cloves of garlic
¼ cup of chopped onions
A small amount of hot peppers of crushed red pepper (optional)
1 – 2 red skin or sweet potatoes sliced or chopped into bit-sized pieces
A handful of green leafy vegetables such as spinach, kale, Swiss chard or collard greens
Handfuls of any variety of vegetable you love such as peppers, mushrooms, zucchini, tomatoes, broccoli, cauliflower or peas
Toppings of choice such as pine nuts, hemp seeds, pumpkin seeds, sliced almonds and/or chopped avocado for healthy fats and protein

Preparation:
Cook the potatoes in the oil until browned and thoroughly cooked. To save time, use leftover cooked potatoes.
Add the onions and garlic and optional hot peppers and cook for several minutes until soft.
Add the remaining veggies and cook lightly, maintaining their color and texture.

Top with nuts and seeds and avocado.

Servings: 2 - 4

Tofu Scramble Ideas
This is a great vegetarian alternative to scrambled eggs.

Ingredients:
1/2 yellow onion, diced
1/2 green bell pepper, diced
1 block tofu, drained and pressed
2 T olive oil
1 tsp garlic powder
1 tsp onion powder
1/2 tsp dried parsley
1 T soy sauce
2 T nutritional yeast
1/2 tsp turmeric
Can add spinach or other veggies as desired

Preparation:
Slice the tofu into approximately one-inch cubes. Then, using either your hands or a fork, crumble it slightly.
Sauté onion, pepper and crumbled tofu in oil for 3-5 minutes, stirring often. Add remaining ingredients, reduce heat to medium and allow to cook for 5-7 more minutes, stirring frequently and adding more oil if needed.
Wrap in a warmed flour tortilla with a bit of salsa for a breakfast burrito or top with soy or rice cheese.

Servings: 4

Curried Tofu Scramble with Spinach

A basic vegetarian and vegan tofu scramble recipe inspired by the flavors of India. Feel free to add some more vegetables, too, such as broccoli or mushrooms.

Ingredients:
1 tsp olive oil
1 onion, diced
3 cloves garlic, minced
1 container firm or extra firm tofu, pressed and crumbled
1 tsp curry powder
1/2 tsp turmeric
1/2 tsp cumin (optional)
salt and pepper to taste
2 tomatoes, diced
1 bunch fresh spinach

Preparation:
Sauté the garlic and onion in olive oil in a large skillet. Allow these to cook for 3 to 5 minutes, or until onion turns soft.
Add remaining ingredients except spinach and cook, stirring frequently for another 5 minutes or so, until tofu is hot and cooked, adding more oil if needed.
Add spinach and cook a minute or two, just until wilted, stirring well.

Servings: 2

Janet McKee Success Coach, Wellness Expert, Speaker and Author
CEO and Founder of SanaView
janet@sanaview.com
©SanaView 2018. All rights reserved.

Banana-Vanilla Pancakes from Janet's book "Mayan Inspired Recipes"

This is from the Mayan Beach Garden, Jardin, Playa Maya.
When I was searching for recipes for the Mayan event I catered, I came across this wonderful alternative to every-day pancakes. Even though I like pancakes, I typically can only eat about one or two. These are different. They are so delicious that I just can't stop eating.

Ingredients:
2 cups all-purpose flour (consider trying 1/2 wholegrain flour or gluten free flours)
1 teaspoon salt
2 1/2 teaspoons double-acting baking powder
1/4 cup sugar or Lakanto (natural zero calorie, zero glycemic sweetener)
1 1/4 cups of non-dairy milk
1/4 cup melted coconut oil or olive oil
2-4 bananas, mashed depending on the size
2 tsp. vanilla ("Mexican Vanilla", if you can find it, is supposed to have an even deeper flavor)
Coconut oil for frying pan or griddle

Janet McKee Success Coach, Wellness Expert, Speaker and Author
CEO and Founder of SanaView
janet@sanaview.com
©SanaView 2018. All rights reserved.

Preparation:
Sift dry ingredients together.
Beat in milk, oil, mashed banana and vanilla.
Make a well in the center of the dry ingredients and pour wet mixture into it.
Quickly stir wet and dry ingredients together until just blended. If too thick, add more milk, a spoonful at a time.

Heat a pan or griddle over medium-low heat and brush with coconut oil. Pour batter by spoonfuls onto the griddle.

Cook until bubbles appear all over the surface. Turn. Top should be evenly browned. Continue cooking until browned on the bottom as well.

Serve with sliced bananas and berries and chopped walnuts for a wonderful meal.

Servings : Makes about a dozen+ medium sized pancakes scooped with a ¼ cup measuring cup.

Janet McKee Success Coach, Wellness Expert, Speaker and Author
CEO and Founder of SanaView
janet@sanaview.com
©SanaView 2018. All rights reserved.

Honey-Vanilla Fruit Compote from Janet's book "Mayan Inspired Recipes"

Recipe by Shanti Morell-Hart who writes: "Vanilla, called t'isil in Mayan, was cultivated throughout Mexico, Guatemala, Honduras, Belize, and El Salvador by the Prehispanic Maya people. Bees were also kept for their honey, which was the type of sweetener most commonly used in the Maya area. The fruits in this recipe are also native to the area and can still be found growing wild in forests, although they may look different from the cultivated varieties we find in supermarkets today."

Ingredients:

3 ½ cups water
1 vanilla bean, split or 1 tablespoon pure vanilla extract
1 ripe medium pineapple, peeled, cored, and diced
10-12 small, ripe, but firm, fresh guavas (optional)
½ pound fresh cherries
sliced grapes for garnish
1 ½ cups honey (optional – I do not believe this is needed)

Our Mayan celebration was taking place during the auspicious time in the Mayan calendar, December 11th, in the eastern part of the United States. Therefore, we incorporated fruits that are commonly found in season at this time of year. We used pears and apples and dried currants. We added some fresh or frozen berries and cherries to add color. It is not necessary to add the honey as the fruit is naturally sweet on their own. This compote can be eaten alone or over a wonderful bowl of cooked grains.

Preparation:

In a three-quart saucepan, combine the honey and water. Place pan over medium heat and bring to a simmer. Stir until the honey is dissolved into a thin syrup.
Place the vanilla bean in the syrup and reduce heat to low.
Bring another large saucepan of water to a boil.
Plunge the guavas into boiling water for a few seconds, then remove and peel.
Add the guavas and cherries to the simmering syrup and poach for 15 minutes, stirring gently from time to time.
Add the pineapple and continue to poach for another 5 minutes.
Turn off heat, and allow the fruit to cool in the syrup and remove the vanilla bean.
Garnish with sliced grapes.

Servings: 4 - 6

Janet McKee Success Coach, Wellness Expert, Speaker and Author
CEO and Founder of SanaView
janet@sanaview.com
©SanaView 2018. All rights reserved.

Raw Cranberry Granola

For those that love to follow the raw food lifestyle approach and want to enjoy a granola that is similar in texture to standard baked granola but still maintains enzymes and nutrients, this is an amazing choice. My entire family loves this for breakfast or just for snacking. I do not add the maple syrup as the dates are sweet enough.

Ingredients:
1 granny smith apple cored and chopped
1 ½ cups of dates or date paste
½ cup maple syrup (optional)
2 T lemon juice
2 T orange zest
1 T vanilla extract
1 tsp ground cinnamon
2 tsp sea salt
½ cup sunflower seeds, soaked for 2 hours
2 cups almonds, soaked for 4 hours
3 cups of pecans or walnuts, soaked for 2 hours
1 cup pumpkin seeds, soaked for 2 hours
1 cup dried cranberries (unsweetened or fruit sweetened if possible)

Janet McKee Success Coach, Wellness Expert, Speaker and Author
CEO and Founder of SanaView
janet@sanaview.com
©SanaView 2018. All rights reserved.

Preparation:
Place the apple, dates, maple syrup (if you choose), lemon juice, orange zest, vanilla, cinnamon, salt and ¼ cup of sunflower seeds and process until smooth.
Place the mixture in a mixing bowl.
Coarsely chop all of the remaining nuts and seeds in the food processor and add them to the mixing bowl and combine.

Spread the mixture on the Teflex-lined dehydrator trays and dehydrate for 115 degrees for 6 - 8 hours.
Flip the granola over onto the screens and peel away the Teflex.
Continue dehydrating for another 8 - 12 hours or until the granola is crunchy.

Break the granola into pieces and store in the refrigerator.
This will stay fresh in the refrigerator for several weeks.

Servings: 4 - 5 sheets worth of granola or 8 - 10 servings

Janet McKee Success Coach, Wellness Expert, Speaker and Author
CEO and Founder of SanaView
janet@sanaview.com
©SanaView 2018. All rights reserved.

HEALTHY SNACKS AND APPETIZERS

The recipe ideas in the breakfast and dessert section of this book can also be used for healthful snacking. All of the foods in this book are wonderfully nourishing and healthy and can be used for meals and for snacking alike. I love to keep an abundance of wonderful choices close at hand that I can grab quickly to satisfy any craving. In addition to satisfying my desire for any variety of tastes or textures, it helps me to feel great knowing that what I am eating is truly good for me.

This is the key to balancing your weight naturally as well. When the foods you choose are high in nutrients and fiber and void of any processed and unhealthy ingredients, you will feel more satisfied because your body is properly nourished. This boosts your metabolism and your mood, which allows your body to balance its weight naturally.

Keeping healthy snacks available is great for family, friends and loved ones too. People are always impressed when they can enjoy something yummy and satisfying that gives them energy and vitality.

Have fun and be creative with ideas. Eating well brings great pleasure at so many levels.

Healthy Snack Ideas:

My clients often say they need ideas for healthy snacks. There are so many wonderful options but I tried to list some key ideas below for quick reference.

Fruit:
- All kinds of colorful and flavorful fresh or frozen or dried fruit
- Frozen bananas taste like banana ice-cream
- Frozen cherries are a wonderful sweet and refreshing treat
- Frozen grapes are fun to munch on
- Fresh Apples, pears or bananas with peanut, almond or any nut butter
- Dried fruit and nuts of choice for a homemade trail mix
- Dried blueberries and cherries taste flavorful, chewy and sweet, just like candy

Dark Chocolate covered strawberries

Coat banana pieces with melted dark chocolate or cocoa powder and roll the banana pieces in chopped nuts or sunflower seeds or coconut and place on wax paper and freeze. Once they are solid, you can put them in a container for storing in the freezer.

Healthy and quick "Ice Cream":
Take one small chunk of frozen banana with one small chunk of frozen fruit of choice (such as strawberry, blueberry, raspberry, peach or mango) and put it through a juicer with a flat screen. Keep repeating until enough "ice cream" is made for you to enjoy. If you don't have a juicer, then put the frozen fruit into a blender with a small amount of non-dairy milk (such as soy, rice, almond, coconut or hemp milk) and blend into a thick and "creamy" treat.

Non-dairy milk shakes and smoothies – see the smoothie section of this book
Place a non-dairy milk of choice in a blender with frozen bananas and other flavorings such as raw cacao, strawberries or peaches.

Celery with Peanut Butter or other nut butter or tahini
You can dot with dried blueberries or raisin for "ants on a log"

Rice Cakes with all kinds of favorite toppings such as nut butter and fruit or fruit juice sweetened jam - or hummus and veggies

Janet McKee Success Coach, Wellness Expert, Speaker and Author
CEO and Founder of SanaView
janet@sanaview.com
©SanaView 2018. All rights reserved.

Popcorn sprinkled with sea salt or nutritional yeast for a "cheesy" flavor

Hummus with veggies and baked tortilla chips or in wraps

Sprouted or gluten free toast with natural fruit juice sweetened jams and/or nut butters

Pickles and/or olives

Salsa and/or Guacamole with veggies and baked tortilla chips

Pretzels

Veggies and healthy "creamy dips" – see recipes under creamy salad dressings

Homemade baked goods with healthy and natural ingredients or see my many healthy dessert ideas including chocolate almond truffles, coconut balls and healthy pies

Homemade fruit popsicles (made with blended fruit smoothies or organic fruit juices)

Baked Yam or Sweet Potato Chips:
   Preheat oven to 350°F. Thinly slice sweet potatoes or yams and place them on a baking sheet. Season the chips as desired with either sea salt or other spicy combinations. Bake for 20 – 25 minutes until cooked through and crisp.
Can also do sweet potato or yam fries.

Edamame – you can find these whole soybeans in the pod in the frozen food section. Simply quick boil and serve with a sprinkling of sea salt

Baked Granola (or see recipe for raw granola):
   Preheat oven to 350°F. Toss rolled oats, nuts, dried fruit with honey and a little olive oil and spread on a baking sheet. Bake in the over for 25 to 30 minutes or until the ingredients are crunchy.

Janet McKee Success Coach, Wellness Expert, Speaker and Author
CEO and Founder of SanaView
janet@sanaview.com
©SanaView 2018. All rights reserved.

Mochi:

This is a Japanese treat made with cooked, pureed rice and contains no wheat or flour. Mochi is found in the refrigerator section of the health food stores and comes in both sweet and savory flavors.

Ball of Nuts:

In a blender, add equal amounts of dates (that have been soaked in water to soften) with rolled oats, almonds, sesame seeds, apple juice, and poppy seeds and blend. Or, a simple form is 2 cups of nuts and ½ cup of soaked dates in a food processor. Form into little balls and refrigerate.

Wheat-free sunflower crunches:

Preheat oven to 375°F. Combine 1 cup of sunflower seeds, ½ cup of sesame seeds, 1 T of poppy seeds and add 1 T of maple syrup with 1 ½ T of olive oil. Roll dough into several long pieces and place them on a lightly oiled baking sheet and bake for 15 – 20 minutes.

Baked Kale Chips (or see recipe for raw kale chips):

Preheat oven to 425°F. Remove the kale from the stems and keep the leaves in large pieces. Place a little olive oil in a bowl, dip your fingers and rub a very light coat of oil over the kale. Lay the kale out on a baking sheet, sprinkle with sea salt and bake for 5 minutes until it starts to turn a bit brown. Turn the kale over and bake the other side.

Confetti Crisps from Real Age:

Take 1 cup each of thinly sliced purple potatoes, carrots and parsnips and coat with 2 T of olive oil, ½ tsp garlic salt, ½ tsp dried dill weed, 1/8 tsp pepper. Arrange in a single layer on a baking sheet that is lightly coated with olive oil. Bake at 350°F for 20 – 25 minutes or until crisp and golden.

See the remaining book for many other healthy snack and dessert ideas and recipes!

Janet McKee Success Coach, Wellness Expert, Speaker and Author
CEO and Founder of SanaView
janet@sanaview.com
©SanaView 2018. All rights reserved.

Fresh Simple Salsa

The following are my own quick and simple salsa and guacamole recipes that do not take much fuss or preparation as the ingredients are simple. They are light and refreshing in taste, without any overpowering flavors, so they go well with any Mexican or Mayan foods you may be serving.

Ingredients:
2 medium tomatoes
2-inch piece of cucumber
2 T of red onion
2 – 3 T of cilantro
Pinch of sea salt (you may optionally add garlic and/or jalapeño peppers)

Preparation:
Place all ingredients in a small food processor until desired combined consistency.

Servings: 6 - 8

Janet McKee Success Coach, Wellness Expert, Speaker and Author
CEO and Founder of SanaView
janet@sanaview.com
©SanaView 2018. All rights reserved.

Guacamole

This recipe is so simple and delicious and provides a great source of healthy fats and nutrients. Use guacamole as a dip, to top burritos, as a spread for wraps and sandwiches or even to top a salad. Serve this with baked tortilla chips, flax crackers or pieces of fresh vegetables such as celery, tomato, red pepper or cucumber.

Ingredients:
2 ripe avocados
Juice of 1/2 lime
¼ cup of cilantro
2 – 3 spring onions
Sea salt to taste – optional

Preparation: Peel avocado and place sections in a bowl. Pour the juice over the avocado, add the cilantro, sliced onions and sea salt and mash together.

Servings: 6 - 8

Janet McKee Success Coach, Wellness Expert, Speaker and Author
CEO and Founder of SanaView
janet@sanaview.com
©SanaView 2018. All rights reserved.

Spinach Almond Dip

Don't be fooled by this unusual mixture of ingredients. This is so good that I always get raving compliments from the crowd when I bring this to parties and gatherings.

Ingredients:
1 bunch of spinach, cleaned and large stems removed
½ cup chopped parsley
2 T almond butter
1 T flax oil
2 T nama shoyu or tamari
1 lemon juiced
1 clove of garlic, pressed or minced

Preparation:
Place all of the ingredients in a food processor and combine into a creamy dip.

Serve this as a dip with vegetables or whole grain crackers and breads. You can use this as a spread for wraps and sandwiches as well.

Servings: 4-6

Black Bean Dip

This recipe is from the book "The Cancer Survivor's Guide" by Neal Barnard, MD. This is so good and so simple and the perfect thing to munch on while watching a football game or movie. The guys will love it too and they will have no idea it is actually healthy for them.

Ingredients:
1 can black beans (or 1 1/2 cups cooked)
1 cup salsa
½ tsp ground cumin

Preparation:
Combine all of the ingredients in a food processor or blender and process until smooth.

Serve with baked tortilla chips and or fresh veggies or use as a filler for bean burritos or tacos. This will keep in the fridge for up to three days.

Servings: 8

Simple Hummus or Roasted Red Pepper Hummus

This recipe is from the book, "The Cancer Survivor's Guide".

Ingredients:

1 ½ cups cooked or canned chickpeas, rinsed and drained (reserve ¼ cup of liquid)
½ cup roasted red bell peppers packed in water, drained (optionally to make roasted red pepper hummus)
3 green onions, sliced
¼ cup freshly squeezed lemon juice
1 T tahini
3 garlic cloves, crushed and minced
1 tsp ground cumin
½ tsp ground black pepper
¼ cup bean cooking liquid, reserved liquid from canned beans or vegetable broth

Janet McKee Success Coach, Wellness Expert, Speaker and Author
CEO and Founder of SanaView
janet@sanaview.com
©SanaView 2018. All rights reserved.

Preparation:
Place all of the ingredients in a food processor or blender and process until smooth. Add the reserved bean liquid or vegetable broth as needed to achieve a smooth consistency.

Serve with cut up veggies or pita bread or crackers or use as a filling for a vegetable wrap.

Hummus will keep in the refrigerator for 3 - 5 days.

Servings: 2 cups or 8 servings

Zucchini Hummus

Sometimes it is nice to have a creamy style dip or spread that is not heavy in beans or nuts. This is a great raw food recipe that is very versatile.

Ingredients:
1 zucchini peeled and chopped (you don't need to peel if the green color is acceptable)
2 T raw tahini
2 T lemon juice
½ tsp crushed garlic (1 clove)
¼ tsp ground cumin
¼ tsp paprika
¼ tsp salt

Preparation:
Place all of the ingredients in a food processor using the S blade and process.
This will keep in the refrigerator for 5 days.

Servings: 4 - 6

Spicy Raw Kale Chips

This is certainly the most nutritious and delicious chips you will ever have! By dehydrating at low temperatures, the kale maintains the maximum nutrients and enzymes. Optionally, you may place these in an oven on low temperatures for a much shorter length of time.

Ingredients:
1 red pepper chopped
1/3 C cashews soaked
¼ C sunflower seeds
Juice of one lemon
1 jalapeno chopped
1 T nutritional yeast
½ tsp salt
1/8 tsp cayenne pepper
2 bunches of kale

Preparation:
Blend all of the ingredients, except for the kale, in a blender or food processor until well blended.
Clean kale and remove the hard stems.
Cut the kale into large pieces and coat with the blended mixture until well coated.

Place in a dehydrator and dehydrate at 115 degrees for 8 to 12 hours until nice and crispy.

Servings: 4 - 6

Raw Kale Chips

This yummy kale chip recipe comes from a local raw food potluck gathering I attended several years ago.

Ingredients:
2 bunches of Kale
¼ cup tahini
¼ cup Apple Cider Vinegar
2 scallions
1 clove garlic
1 lemon juiced
¼ cup nutritional yeast

Preparation:
Combine all of the ingredients above, except the kale, in a blender or food processor until the mixture is a thick consistency.
Pour the blended mixture on cleaned and de-veined kale and mix to coat evenly.

Place on dehydrator sheets at 115°F for 6 hrs.

When complete, sprinkle with sunflower seeds or sesame seeds and sprinkle with salt and serve.

Servings: 6 - 8

Janet McKee Success Coach, Wellness Expert, Speaker and Author
CEO and Founder of SanaView
janet@sanaview.com
©SanaView 2018. All rights reserved.

Raw Nori Rolls

This is another simple raw food dish that I either cut into small rounds and serve it as a beautiful appetizer or I cut each roll in half lengthwise and eat them as hand rolls for lunch. The nori rolls are definitely one of my favorites as they are a quick and satisfying alternative to a salad.

Use cooked brown rice or quinoa for a non-raw nori roll alternative.

Ingredients:
Jicama (peel & cube) or cauliflower cut into chunks
Spinach
Tomatoes (chopped small)
Cucumber
Avocados (sliced)
Broccoli sprouts
Nori Sheets (untoasted)
Flax oil and sea salt (optional)

Preparation:
Place jicama or cauliflower in a food processor and chop into a rice consistency.
You may drizzle the "rice" with a bit of flax oil and sea salt if you so choose.

Spread the "rice" mixture onto a nori sheet then layer with spinach, avocado, tomato, cucumber, sprouts or any vegetable of choice.

Roll nori to make it like a California roll. Seal the edge with a bit of water to keep it together.
At this point you can either cut in half for 2 larger rolls, or cut into about 6 bite size pieces.

Serve with Braggs Liquid Aminos or Nama Shoyu or Tamari and perhaps some wasabi to possibly give it more of a sushi taste.

Servings: 8 - 10 rolls depending on the size of the jicama root

Raw Collard Green Wraps

This is a great, beautiful and fun vegetable wrap to serve to guests. The big ears of the collard plant are perfect for stuffing with your favorite vegetables. Be creative and enjoy!

Ingredients:
2 cups of raw walnuts
1 cup sun dried tomatoes, soaked in water until soft
¼ cup olive oil or flax oil
1 T of water
1 T of Nama Shoyu or Tamari soy sauce or Bragg's Liquid Aminos
1 clove of garlic
Spices of choice such as cayenne and cumin to taste
A bunch of collard greens

Preparation:
Place walnuts in a food processor or blender and blend until it forms a powdery consistency.
Transfer the walnut powder for a mixing bowl.

Blend the rest of the ingredients in the food processor or blender and stir the mixture into the walnuts powder.

Spread the walnut/tomato mixture thinly on a collard green leaf with the hard stem removed. Add any favorite raw vegetables such as cucumbers, red peppers, carrots and sprouts. Roll it up and secure with a toothpick and enjoy!

A **simple alternative** is to load collard greens with any veggies along with either hummus or a simple tahini dressing, roll into a wrap and enjoy.

Servings: 6 - 8

Janet McKee Success Coach, Wellness Expert, Speaker and Author
CEO and Founder of SanaView
janet@sanaview.com
©SanaView 2018. All rights reserved.

Raw Curried Almonds

By soaking nuts, you release the enzyme inhibitors that can make nuts sometimes hard to digest. Once nuts are soaked, the texture is softer and they need to be stored in the fridge or they will go bad quickly. If you dehydrate the nuts after soaking, they become crunchy again without harming the enzymes or adversely affecting the fats. These are so good!

Ingredients:
2 cups raw almonds, soaked for 4 – 6 hours
2 tsp curry powder
¾ tsp cumin powder
2 – 3 T olive oil
2 tsp lemon juice
1 tsp agave nectar, honey or Lakanto
½ tsp sea salt

Preparation:
Drain and rinse soaked almonds and place in a large bowl with remaining ingredients.

Toss well to coat the almonds with the seasoning.

Pour nuts onto a Teflex-lined dehydrator sheet and dehydrate at 115°F for 6 – 8 hours or until most of the liquid on the tray has dried.

Transfer the nuts onto unlined screens and dehydrate overnight until crisp.

Servings: 8 ¼ cup servings

HEART WARMING SOUPS AND STEWS

Ah – there is nothing more wonderful than a heart and soul warming and nourishing soup or stew on a cold fall or winter evening. These are the easiest and most fabulous ways to get family members, especially kids, to eat a wide variety of plentiful vegetables and beans. Stews are wonderful served over delicious whole grains, such as brown rice, quinoa or millet to round out a perfect hearty meal.

The trick to improve the taste and texture of some vegetable soups is to puree them in the blender once they are done cooking. This makes it appear creamier and thicker which is satisfying for everyone without adding unhealthy ingredients such as high fat dairy. By blending the vegetables too, it makes them more appealing to some who don't favor a mouth full of broccoli etc. You may use the "farmer's market broccoli soup" recipe as a basic soup for inspiration. Add whatever vegetables you have on hand and create your own recipe.

Many of our family favorites are found in this section. I am sure they will become some of your family's favorites too, so enjoy!

Farmer's Market Fresh Broccoli Soup

One of my good friends and I visited the farmers market one fall day on Long Island, NY and purchased fresh vegetables that were in season. We combined what we bought into this wonderful soup that we both enjoy often throughout the fall and winter. Use any vegetable that is in season to combine with the broccoli. I assure you; it too will become a favorite in your home.

Ingredients:
1 small to medium sized onion finely chopped
1 large or 3 small leeks cut in half lengthwise and sliced
2 large cloves of garlic chopped
1 T coconut oil
10 cups water with 4 good quality vegetable bouillon
Or
Any combination of water with vegetable broth to taste
Sea salt to taste
Black pepper to taste
1 head of broccoli chopped

Janet McKee Success Coach, Wellness Expert, Speaker and Author
CEO and Founder of SanaView
janet@sanaview.com
©SanaView 2018. All rights reserved.

4 – 6 small red skin potatoes
1 large carrot chopped
½ butternut squash seeded and chopped
Hand full of fresh Brussels sprouts, green beans, zucchini or any other chopped vegetable of choice

Preparation:
Sauté the onion, leeks and garlic in the coconut oil for a few minutes until soft. Add the remaining ingredients, bring to a boil, turn down the heat and simmer for 30 minutes.

Transfer the soup to a blender or use an immersion blender to blend. This makes the soup creamier and less chunky. Leave a few chunks of vegetables in the soup for color and texture.

Servings: 8

Asparagus Soup

This recipe was inspired by from the January 2004 issue of Taste for Life. This is an elegant and wonderfully tasty soup that you simply must try.

Ingredients:
1 small leek sliced
1 bunch of chopped asparagus (remove tough ends by snapping off) and chop
2 celery stalks chopped
Zest of one lemon
2 cups of non-dairy milk such as soy, rice or almond milk
2 cups spring or filtered water
2 T mirin rice wine or white wine (optional!!)
Sea salt to taste
Hempseeds to garnish

Preparation:
Place all of the ingredients, except for hemp seeds, in a soup pot. Bring the soup to a light boil, reduce the heat and simmer for 15 minutes.

Transfer the soup to a blender and puree until smooth.
Return the soup to the pot, add more sea salt if necessary, and simmer for 2 more minutes.

Garnish generously with hemp seeds and serve.

Servings: 4

Creamy Cauliflower Potato Soup

I found this recipe in my box of recipes and simply can't recall the source, but it is incredibly delicious. It takes like a flavorful potato soup and you will have no idea that it is actually mostly cauliflower, which is more nutritious.

Ingredients:
2 T of coconut oil
1 medium onion diced
2 cloves garlic minced
1 head of cauliflower cut into small pieces
1 medium red-skin potato chopped
2 stalks of celery chopped
1 bay leaf
6 cups of vegetable broth
½ tsp nutmeg
Sea salt and pepper to taste
Cayenne pepper to taste (optional)
Finely chopped red pepper and parsley to garnish

Preparation:
Heat the oil over medium heat. Add the onion, garlic and sea salt and sauté until the onion is soft; about ten minutes.
Add the cauliflower, potato, celery, bay leaf and broth. Bring to a boil, then lower the heat and simmer covered for 30 minutes until the cauliflower is tender.
Puree the soup in a blender or use a hand immersion blender to blend until smooth and creamy.
Return the soup to the pot and add the nutmeg, cayenne and additional salt and pepper if needed.
Garnish and serve.

Servings: 6

Miso Soup

This recipe is inspired by and adapted from my favorite restaurant in NYC, Angelica's Kitchen. The wakame and kombu are sea vegetables that can be found in the Asian section of the grocery or health food store and provide wonderful nutrients.

Ingredients:

1 small piece of Wakame soaked in water for 15 minutes until soft
1 3 - 4 inch of Kombu
4 cups of water
1 carrot chopped into bite sized pieces
1 stalk of celery cut into bite sized pieces
1 small onion sliced
Additional chopped greens or cabbage as you desire
Chopped shitake mushrooms
4 tablespoons of miso (may add more or less according to your taste - do not overdo)
1 cup of tofu (optional)
Add parsley and or scallions for garnish.

Janet McKee Success Coach, Wellness Expert, Speaker and Author
CEO and Founder of SanaView
janet@sanaview.com
©SanaView 2018. All rights reserved.

Preparation:
Put the kombu in 4 cups of water and simmer for a few minutes. Remove the kombu from the water. Chop the wakame and add along with the soaking water and the chopped vegetables to the soup pot. Bring the soup to a simmer, cover and cook for 15 - 20 minutes. Dissolve the miso into approximately a cup of the soup stock and add it back to the pot. If using tofu, add to the soup and simmer for 1 -2 minutes being careful not to boil the soup as it will harm the benefits of the miso. Garnish and serve.

Servings: 2 - 4

Simple Vegetable Noodle Soup Option

This is a quick and simple soup that can be made in a pinch using any vegetables you have in the fridge.
Cook all of the above vegetables in vegetable broth instead of using miso.
Optionally add cooked rice or uncooked rice noodles and simmer for 5 minutes until soft.

Raw Creamy Miso Soup

This recipe was inspired and adapted from a recipe by Viktoras Kulvinskas. This is probably one of the most delicious yet healing, nourishing and detoxifying soups.

Ingredients:
1 cup of sesame seeds
6 cups water
1 – 2 stalks of celery
¼ - ½ red onion
1 lemon juiced
1 small bunch of cilantro
1 tsp salt
2 T tahini
2 T red or mellow miso
1 cup kelp cut into small pieces

Preparation:

First make the sesame milk by soaking the sesame seeds approximately 8 hours.

Rinse and drain the sesame seeds and add to a blender with the water. After the seeds and water are blended well, strain through a nut milk bag. Reserve the sesame milk and discard the solids.

Add the remaining ingredients, except the kelp, to the blender with the nut milk and blend.

Soak the kelp in warm water to soften. Drain the kelp and add to the soup. This can be enjoyed cold or warmed slightly.

Servings: 4 - 6

Lentil Soup

This recipe is from the book, "The Cancer Survivor's Guide".

Ingredients:
1 cup of dry lentils, rinsed
5 cups of vegetable broth or water
1 onion, chopped
1 stalk celery, chopped
1 potato, chopped
2 cloves of garlic, minced
1 tsp ground cumin
1 tsp ground coriander
1 cup crushed tomatoes
½ cup chopped fresh cilantro
1/8 tsp black pepper
½ tsp salt or to taste
Juice of one lemon

Preparation:
Combine lentils, broth or water, onion, celery, potato, and garlic in a large pot. Cover and simmer 30 minutes.

Toast the cumin and coriander in a dry skillet over high heat, stirring constantly, until fragrant, about 30 seconds.

Add to lentils along with tomatoes, cilantro, and black pepper. Simmer 15 minutes. Add salt to taste. Stir in lemon juice before serving.

Servings: 6 - 8

Butternut Squash Soup with Fried Sage Leaves

Adapted from Bon Appetit, Flavors of the World

Ingredients:
3 T coconut oil
1 onion, coarsely chopped
1 T chopped fresh sage
1 2 ¾ pound squash, halved, seeded, chopped (about 5 cups)
5 cups of vegetable broth
1/3 cup vegan Parmesan or nutritional yeast (optional)
24 fresh sage leaves

Preparation:
Melt 1 tablespoon of coconut oil in a heavy large pot over medium heat.

Add onion; cover and cook until soft, stirring occasionally, about 7 minutes.
Add chopped sage, stir 1 minute.
Add squash and broth. Increase heat to high and bring to a boil.

Janet McKee Success Coach, Wellness Expert, Speaker and Author
CEO and Founder of SanaView
janet@sanaview.com
©SanaView 2018. All rights reserved.

Reduce heat and simmer until squash is tender, about 25 minutes.
Cool slightly.

Puree soup in batches in a blender until smooth.
Return the soup to the pot and mix in the cheese.
Season to taste with salt and pepper
(this can be made one day ahead, cool slightly then cover and refrigerate)

Melt 2 tablespoons of coconut oil in a heavy large skillet over medium heat.
Add sage leaves and sauté until brown and toasted about 2 minutes.

Bring the soup to a simmer again.

Ladle into bowls and garnish with fried sage leaves.

Servings: 8

Butternut Squash and Red Bell Pepper Soup with Ginger and Hemp Seeds
Inspired by Manitoba Harvest

Ingredients:
1 T olive oil or coconut oil
3 large leeks
1 large butternut squash
¼ large red bell pepper
6 cups of vegetable broth
4 T fresh-grated ginger
2 cups hemp seeds
1 T cayenne pepper (optional)

Preparation:
Cut squash into large sections and remove the ends and seeds. Bake the squash in a roasting pan at 350 for 45 minutes or until fork tender.

While squash is baking, chop leeks and red pepper and combine with a pinch of grated ginger in a large pan with the oil and sauté on medium heat for a few minutes until soft.

Scoop out the soft butternut squash and add to the pan with the leeks and simmer for about 5 minutes.

Warm vegetable broth in another pot and add to the squash mixture one cup at a time until creamy and thick. Transfer the squash mixture and any remaining stock along with the cayenne and hemp seeds and blend until creamy. Garnish with additional hemp seeds and serve.

Servings: 6

Janet McKee Success Coach, Wellness Expert, Speaker and Author
CEO and Founder of SanaView
janet@sanaview.com
©SanaView 2018. All rights reserved.

Raw Butternut Squash Soup

Yes, butternut squash can be eaten raw! This recipe is adapted from Dr. Gabriel Cousens of the Tree of Life Rejuvenation Center by my friend David Dreyfus.

Ingredients:

2 C butternut squash peeled and cubed
1 Red bell pepper seeded and chopped
2 Stalks of celery
1 Tomato
1 Small Leek
2 T Parsley
2 T Cilantro
1 T Flax Oil
2 ½ C Water
1 tsp Sea Salt
½ tsp Cinnamon
¼ tsp black pepper
dash of cayenne

Janet McKee Success Coach, Wellness Expert, Speaker and Author
CEO and Founder of SanaView
janet@sanaview.com
©SanaView 2018. All rights reserved.

Preparation:
Combine all of the ingredients in a blender and blend until smooth. You may blend until slightly warm if you choose. Garnish with more parsley and cilantro.

Servings: 4 - 6

Hearty Vegetable and Grain Soup

One of my best friends fed this soup to me once while in NY studying at the Integrative Institute and again during one weekend visit to VT. This is certain to become one of your cold-weather favorites.

Ingredients:

1 tsp coconut oil
1 whole yellow onion chopped
4 – 6 cloves of garlic chopped
1 T Italian season blend
1 tsp dry parsley
1 T dried basil
12 cups water
½ bundle of broccoli chopped
Zucchini or yellow squash chopped
1 Large yam chopped
1 cup of quinoa rinsed and drained.
½ cup whole leaf kelp cut into small pieces

Janet McKee Success Coach, Wellness Expert, Speaker and Author
CEO and Founder of SanaView
janet@sanaview.com
©SanaView 2018. All rights reserved.

1 28 oz can of crushed tomatoes
1 jar 7 oz jar of tomato paste
1 - 2 cups chopped collards and kale
1 tsp sea salt

Preparation:
Sauté onion and garlic in oil in a large soup pot until onion is translucent. Add the water, chopped vegetables, kelp, tomatoes, and quinoa, bring to a boil and simmer for 30 minutes.

It is recommended to add the stems of the kale and collards early with the other vegetables and add the chopped green leafy parts during the last few minutes of the cooking time to prevent over cooking. Also, add the sea salt after cooking is complete and before serving. Stir to dissolve.

Servings: 8

Carrot Ginger Soup

The liberal amount of ginger in this soup is good for soothing inflammation or digestive discomfort. The remaining ingredients are high in antioxidants and phytonutrients to help fight cancer and other illnesses as well.

Ingredients:
1 T extra virgin olive oil
1 medium red onion, diced
2 T minced fresh ginger
3 cloves garlic, minced
1 pound carrots, peeled and chopped
3 cups vegetable broth
¼ cup orange juice
¼ tsp salt
1/8 tsp pepper

Preparation:
Heat olive oil over medium heat in the bottom of soup pot.
Add the diced onion and cook until soft, stirring occasionally, but do not brown.
Add the ginger and garlic, stir, and cook until fragrant, about 1 minute.
Add the carrots, broth, orange juice, salt and pepper.
Stir all the ingredients together.

Bring to a boil, then reduce heat and simmer until carrots are very tender, about 20-30 minutes.
In batches, puree soup in blender (or do it in the pot if you have an immersion blender).

Thin with additional broth as needed. Taste for seasoning and add a bit more salt if needed.

Servings: 4

Chickpea and Spinach Soup
From Dr. Julia Greer's Anticancer Cookbook

Ingredients:
2 T olive oil
4 cloves of garlic, minced
¼ cup finely chopped shallots
1/3 cup diced celery
Pinch of red pepper flakes
4 cups of vegetable stock
1 ½ T finely chopped fresh rosemary
1 15-ounce can of garbanzo beans
1 ¼ cups cooked brown rice
1 cup of diced tomatoes
Sea salt and freshly ground black pepper to taste
2 cups of fresh chopped spinach

Preparation:
Sauté the garlic and shallots in olive oil in a large soup pot for 1 - 2 minutes.
Add celery and red pepper flakes and continue to sauté for another 1 - 2 minutes.
Add vegetable stock, rosemary, chickpeas, rice, tomatoes and salt.
Cover and bring to a boil.
Reduce heat to medium low and simmer about 30 minutes.

Pour about half of the soup into a blender and blend to make the soup creamier.
Return the blended soup to the pot.
Season with salt and pepper and add chopped spinach.
Simmer on low heat for 6 or 7 minutes and serve hot.

Servings: 6

Janet McKee Success Coach, Wellness Expert, Speaker and Author
CEO and Founder of SanaView
janet@sanaview.com
©SanaView 2018. All rights reserved.

Vegetarian Split Pea Soup

I sometimes throw a couple handfuls of broccoli or spinach into this soup a few minutes before doing the puree.

Ingredients:
1 T extra virgin olive oil
2 large onions, chopped
1/2 teaspoon sea salt
2 cups dried split green peas, picked over and rinsed
5 cups vegetable broth
juice of 1/2 lemon (reserve the zest)
a few pinches of smoked paprika
more olive oil to drizzle

Preparation:
Add olive oil to a big pot over med-high heat.
Stir in onions and salt and cook until the onions soften, just a minute or two.
Add the split peas and water.
Bring to a boil, dial down the heat, and simmer for 20 minutes, or until the peas are cooked through (but still a touch *al dente*).

Using a large cup or mug ladle half of the soup into a bowl and set aside.
Using a hand blender (or regular blender) puree the soup that is still remaining in the pot. Stir the reserved (still chunky) soup back into the puree - you should have a soup that is nicely textured.

If you need to thin the soup out with more water (or stock) do so a bit at a time. Stir in the lemon juice and taste. If the soup needs more salt, add more a bit at a time until the flavor of the soup really pops.
Ladle into bowls or cups, and serve each drizzled with olive oil and topped with a good pinch of smoked paprika and a touch of lemon zest.

Serves 4 to 6

Janet McKee Success Coach, Wellness Expert, Speaker and Author
CEO and Founder of SanaView
janet@sanaview.com
©SanaView 2018. All rights reserved.

Curried Broccoli Soup

This is a super simple way to enjoy the taste and health benefits of broccoli and curry.

Ingredients:
1 T extra-virgin olive oil or coconut oil
½ large or 1 medium onion diced
1 head of broccoli
Almond milk made without honey and less water for thicker consistency or any non-dairy milk
1 package of shiitake mushrooms (optional)
Sea salt and freshly ground pepper
Curry powder (mild or hot depending on taste preference)

Preparation:
Chop the broccoli into smaller pieces and lightly steam until soft but still bright green.
While the broccoli is steaming, be sure to sauté the onion (and mushrooms if you choose) in the oil until tender.
Process the broccoli and onion mixture in a food processor with as much milk as you desire to achieve the preferred consistency.
Add the salt, pepper and curry to taste.

Servings: 4 - 6

Curried Zucchini Soup

This is a nice variation to the previous curried broccoli soup recipe, especially when zucchini is abundantly available in mid to late summer.

Ingredients:
1 large onion peeled, halved and cut into thin slices
2 T extra-virgin olive oil
1 T curry powder or to taste
Sea salt to taste
4 small zucchinis cut lengthwise and crosswise into 1" pieces
1 quart of vegetable stock

Preparation:
In a heavy saucepan, combine onion, oil, curry, and salt.
Stir to coat the onions. Cook over low heat, stirring until the onions are soft, about 3 - 4 minutes.
Add zucchini and cook until soft, about 3 - 4 minutes.
Add the stock and stir to blend.
Bring to a simmer over medium heat, cover and simmer for 20 minutes. Remove the pot from the heat.
Puree soup in a blender or by using a hand immersion blender.

Servings: 6 - 8

Potato and Winter Greens Soup

The guys in my family really enjoy this soup on a crisp fall day.

Ingredients:
4 T extra virgin olive oil or coconut oil
2 medium leeks, white and light green parts chopped and rinsed
5 large red skinned potatoes, thinly sliced
1 large garlic clove minced
4 cups of vegetable broth
1 pound of kale, collards, or mustard greens remove stems and thinly slice
Sea salt and pepper to taste

Preparation:
Heat 3 tablespoons of oil in a large saucepan over medium heat.
Add leaks, cover and cook lightly until soft, about 10 minutes. Add potatoes and sauté until browned, about another 10 minutes.
Add garlic and cook about 1 minute.
Add broth and 4 cups of water.
Bring to a boil, lower heat, cover and simmer for about 20 minutes until potatoes are soft.
Remove from heat and lightly mash the potatoes by hand.

Add the greens to the pot and simmer for about 5 minutes until the greens are tender but still bright green.

Season to taste with salt and pepper and serve.

Servings: 4 - 6

Tomato Basil Soup

This is adapted from "The Simply Great Cookbook: Recipes and the Experience of Fine Dining from the Kitchens of Chuck Muer". I make several pots of this in late summer when I am inundated with more tomatoes than I can possibly eat and the basil is fresh and aromatic. I freeze half so that we can enjoy the tastes of summer mid-winter when we are knee deep in snow and ice.

Ingredients:

¼ cup of olive oil
1 cup of celery, finely diced
1 cup of onions, finely diced
1 cup of carrots, finely diced
4 T of fresh basil or 1tsp dried
1 T of fresh oregano or 1 tsp dried
½ bay leaf
3 cups of whole tomatoes ground in a food processor with juice
4 cups of vegetable broth (or water with two large vegetable bouillon cubes)
2 cups of rice, soy or nut milk
¼ tsp ground white pepper
1 tsp salt

Janet McKee Success Coach, Wellness Expert, Speaker and Author
CEO and Founder of SanaView
janet@sanaview.com
©SanaView 2018. All rights reserved.

Preparation:
Heat oil in a 4-quart soup pot.
Add celery, onions and carrots and sauté for 5 minutes.
Add basil, oregano and bay leaf. Add ground tomatoes and broth.
Bring the soup to a boil, simmer and cook for 15 minutes until carrots are tender.

Warm the non-dairy milk in a pot.
Add warm milk and season with salt and white pepper.

Simmer soup gently for 15 – 20 minutes.

Servings: 8

Sweet and Spicy Squash Soup
Varied flavors make this soup interesting.

Ingredients:
1 T extra virgin olive oil or coconut oil
1 winter squash such as butternut, acorn, pumpkin or delicate seeded and chopped
1 onion minced
2 cloves of garlic minced
Vegetable broth
2 tsp curry powder
1 ½ tsp cumin
Chopped fresh cilantro or parsley or pumpkin seeds for garnish

Preparation:
Sauté the onion and garlic in oil until soft.
Add squash, spices, and enough broth to cover and boil until tender.
Mash or blend in a blender until smooth and simmer for a few more minutes to heat through.

Servings: 4

Janet McKee Success Coach, Wellness Expert, Speaker and Author
CEO and Founder of SanaView
janet@sanaview.com
©SanaView 2018. All rights reserved.

Raw Seventh Heaven Soup

This is an amazing healing soup from Dr. Jubb who is a raw food doctor located in Manhattan.

Ingredients:
¼ cup freshly ground sesame seed (or 4 T raw tahini)
½ cucumber with peel
1 red pepper, cored and deseeded
1 medium tomato
½ cup lemon juice
1 T ginger root, peeled and chopped
3 whole cloves of garlic, peeled
¼ cup red onion, chopped
1 1/2 cup cilantro, chopped and loosely packed
2 T miso
2 T Braggs Liquid Aminos or nama shoyu or tamari
4 T olive or flax oil
¼ tsp cayenne pepper (or to taste)
Salt and pepper to taste
1 T nutritional yeast
2 ½ cups of water

Preparation:
Grind the sesame seed in a spice grinder.
Chop all of the vegetables and put them in a blender and blend.

Garnish with spirulina or dulse and enjoy.

You may store this in the refrigerator for up to 36 hours.

Servings: 4

Janet McKee Success Coach, Wellness Expert, Speaker and Author
CEO and Founder of SanaView
janet@sanaview.com
©SanaView 2018. All rights reserved.

Lentil Artichoke Stew

This recipe is from the book, "The Cancer Survivor's Guide".
This is absolutely a favorite of my family and my clients alike as it is so simple and so good.

Ingredients:
1/4 cup vegetable broth
2 onions, chopped
2 large garlic cloves, pressed or minced
2 teaspoons ground cumin
1 teaspoon ground coriander
1 cup dry (uncooked) red lentils (3 cups cooked)
1 bay leaf
2 cups water
juice of 1 lemon
2 24-ounce jars of chopped tomatoes (preferably fire-roasted), undrained, or 6 cups freshly chopped tomatoes plus 1 cup tomato juice
1 1/2 cups quartered artichoke hearts (1 9-ounce frozen package or 1 15-ounce jar)
1/4 teaspoon crushed red pepper (optional)
1/4 teaspoon salt, or to taste
1/4 teaspoon black pepper, or to taste

Preparation:
Heat broth in a large saucepan.
Add onion and sauté on medium heat for about 5 minutes, until golden.
Add garlic, cumin, and coriander and cook for 2 minutes, stirring frequently.
Add dried lentils, bay leaf, and water to pan and bring to a boil.
Lower heat and add lemon juice, tomatoes and their liquid, artichokes, and crushed red pepper (if using). Simmer for about 20 minutes, until the lentils are tender.

Remove and discard the bay leaf.
Add salt and black pepper, or to taste

Servings: 6

Janet McKee Success Coach, Wellness Expert, Speaker and Author
CEO and Founder of SanaView
janet@sanaview.com
©SanaView 2018. All rights reserved.

Quinoa and Vegetable Stew

I adapted this recipe originally from the Moosewood Dairy. Quinoa is a wonderful gluten free grain and a wonderful source of protein. Quinoa and vegetables are a perfect combination to many soups and stews.

Ingredients:

½ cup quinoa
2 T olive or coconut oil
2 cups chopped onions
1 tsp sea salt
1 cup diced red skin potatoes, sweet potatoes or yams
1 cup chopped sweet pepper
1 cup chopped winter squash such as acorn or butternut (optional)
1 tsp ground coriander
1 tsp ground cumin
1 tsp dried oregano
½ tsp pepper
6 cups water or vegetable broth
1 14oz jar of crushed tomatoes (or chopped fresh tomatoes)
1 cup diced zucchini or yellow squash
1 T lemon juice

Janet McKee Success Coach, Wellness Expert, Speaker and Author
CEO and Founder of SanaView
janet@sanaview.com
©SanaView 2018. All rights reserved.

Preparation:
Thoroughly rinse and drain the quinoa in a fine mesh strainer.
Heat oil in a soup pot and add the onions and salt and cover to cook on medium for 5 minutes, stirring occasionally.
Add the quinoa, potatoes, peppers, spices, water or stock, and tomatoes.
Cover and bring to a boil.
Reduce the heat and simmer gently for 10 minutes.
Add squash and cover and simmer for 15 - 20 minutes, or until all veggies are tender.

Stir in lemon juice.

Serve with optional garnishes: chopped scallions, fresh cilantro, crumbled tortilla chips etc.

Servings: 4 - 6

Vegetable Stew with Spicy Sauce and Grains

This recipe is from my mother, Henrietta Ruberto.
This is a staple recipe in my home for the fall and winter. The entire family loves this vegetarian meal. The dish is hearty and satisfying, healthy and absolutely delicious. We serve hot sauce on the side so that each member of the family can determine the degree of spice they prefer. I like to serve this with quinoa because it is very high in protein and it gives me the option to eliminate the beans on occasion.

Ingredients:
Stew:
2 T cup olive oil
1 large onion, finely chopped
1 each large red and green pepper, seeded and chopped
1 tsp ground coriander
½ tsp ground cinnamon
2 medium-size sweet potatoes or yams cut into ½ inch cubes
2 large tomatoes, chopped
¼ cup water
1 T lemon juice
½ tsp saffron threads
2 cups cooked, drained garbanzo beans (optional)
Sea salt
1 medium zucchini chopped
4 cups of hot cooked grains such as quinoa, millet, brown rice, or couscous

Hot pepper sauce:
1/4 cup olive oil
2 ½ tsp cayenne pepper
1 ½ tsp ground cumin
1 clove minced garlic
¼ tsp salt

Preparation:
Heat oil in a 5-quart pot over medium heat.
Add onion, red and green bell peppers, coriander, and cinnamon and cook, stirring occasionally, until onion is soft (about 5 minutes).
Stir in sweet potatoes and cook, stirring often for 2 minutes.
Add tomatoes, water, lemon juice, saffron, and garbanzos.
Season to taste with salt.
Cover, reduce heat, and simmer 15 minutes more.

Meanwhile, prepare hot pepper sauce.
In a small pan, combine all of the ingredients and cook over medium-low heat, stirring until ingredients are well blended (about 5 minutes).
Serve warm. Makes about ½ cup.

After the stew has cooked for 15 minutes, mix zucchini into the mixture and cook, covered, until sweet potatoes are tender (about 5 minutes more).
Add more salt if desired.

To serve, put grains in each bowl and top with stew and hot sauce. Or, put stew in the center of a deep platter and spread the grains around the edge. Pass the hot pepper sauce to drizzle on top.

Servings: 6

Simplest Ever Black Bean Chili

This is a recipe adapted from the Physician's Committee for Responsible Medicine as part of the Food For Life class on Reversing Diabetes. You can do the gourmet thing and make everything from scratch but if you want something healthy and super quick, try this simple yet amazing dish. This is great for large crowds since it is so easy to make. Be sure to serve it over brown rice or quinoa and accompany with a green salad for a nice hearty satisfying meal.

Ingredients:

2 25-ounce can of organic black beans drained.
2 16-ounce jars of any organic salsa you love
1 16-ounce bag of frozen organic corn
Optional
Juice of two limes
¼ cup of cilantro
chopped avocado
Add cumin and salt and pepper to taste

Janet McKee Success Coach, Wellness Expert, Speaker and Author
CEO and Founder of SanaView
janet@sanaview.com
©SanaView 2018. All rights reserved.

Preparation:
Combine beans, salsa and corn in a pot and cook for 20 - 30 minutes until heated through.

Optionally add a bit of lime juice and garnish with cilantro and avocado before serving.

Serves 8 - 10

Janet's Vegetable Coconut Curry

I took several recipe ideas that I found online and created my own incredibly good vegetable curry. You must try this one!

Ingredients:
2 cups of rice
2 tablespoons olive or coconut oil
1 large onion, chopped
Sea salt and freshly ground black pepper
2 teaspoons curry powder
2 cloves garlic, chopped
1 cup vegetable stock
1 16 oz bag of frozen peas or 1 can of chick peas
½ - 1 large cauliflower cut into small florets (or any vegetable you choose such as broccoli, red sweet peppers etc…)
1.5 – 2 cups of coconut milk
1 to 2 tablespoons sriracha sauce
Chopped fresh cilantro, for garnish.

Preparation:
Cook the rice according to the package instructions.
Heat the oil in a medium skillet over medium-low heat. Add the onions, season with salt and pepper and cook until the onions are dark brown and caramelized, about 10 minutes. Stir in the curry powder and garlic and cook for 30 seconds. Pour in the vegetable stock and stir to scrape up all the brown bits in the pan. Add the vegetables, coconut milk, and a squirt of sriracha. Bring to a boil, reduce the heat and simmer for 10 minutes. Taste and adjust the seasoning.

Serve the curry over the rice. Garnish with the cilantro.

Servings: 4 - 6

Janet McKee Success Coach, Wellness Expert, Speaker and Author
CEO and Founder of SanaView
janet@sanaview.com
©SanaView 2018. All rights reserved.

SUMPTUOUS SALADS AND VEGETABLE SIDE DISHES

Include a beautiful colorful salad to your diet every day and your health will improve by leaps and bounds. Now, many of you know that I am referring to more than a bowl of iceberg lettuce and a high fat dairy dressing. What I am referring to here is an amazing assortment of deep leafy greens, red tomatoes, cabbage or beats, yellow and orange carrots, squash and peppers, and a wide assortment of onions, garlic, herbs and spices to give it amazing flavor and nutrients.

Get creative here too so that you don't get bored. The key is the dressing. So, I have compiled a list of tasty interesting salad dressing ideas to delight your palate while enjoying a bowl of beautiful fresh vegetables.

Some of these dressings are great on steamed and sautéed greens and other vegetables as well. Include several options to accompany other foods and you will discover that you have created an amazing feast for the eyes as well as the stomach.

Enjoy the abundance that Mother Nature has on offer to you. You will be grateful for the results you see in your health, vitality, body image and longevity.

Salad Dressings

OK – the perfect way to bring in wonderful healthful fresh veggies into your daily diet is by including delicious and varied salads. The key is to play around with different dressings and experimenting with a wide variety of veggies to keep from getting bored.

Simple oil and vinegar:
Combine:
6 T olive oil or flax oil or combination of the two
2 – 3 T apple cider vinegar (or other vinegar)
1 tsp sea salt (or to taste)

Simple Lemon and Oil:
Combine:
¼ cup olive or flax oil
juice and zest from 1 lemon
1 tsp salt and ¼ tsp pepper

French Dressing Alternative:
Combine:
4 T flaxseed oil
2 T lemon juice
1 tsp honey or maple syrup
1 tsp nama shoyu (unpasteurized soy sauce), or tamari (wheat-free soy sauce), or sea salt

Avocado Orange Dressing:
Combine:
Juice of one orange
1 avocado chopped
1 tsp sea salt
Simple add on top of a bowl of greens and toss

Fruity Dressing:
Combine:
¼ cup lemon juice
2 tsp chopped fresh mint
¾ tsp cumin
Dash cayenne

Oil Free Blueberry Dressing:
Blend:
1 cup blueberries
½ cup water
2 T apple juice concentrate (or orange juice concentrate)
1 T apple cider vinegar
1 T lemon juice
1 tsp sea salt

Pineapple-Ginger Dressing:
Combine:
1 cup fresh pineapple juice
1 tsp fresh ginger juice
1 T sesame oil or flax oil

"Creamy" Dressings:

Honey Mustard Dressing:
Blend:
½ cup olive oil
¼ cup apple cider vinegar or lemon juice
1 T Dijon mustard
2 tsp raw honey
½ tsp sea salt
½ tsp crushed garlic or 1 clove
Dash black pepper

Creamy Cucumber Dressing:
Blend:
1 small cucumber peeled and seeded and chopped
¼ cup olive oil
1 ½ T fresh lemon juice
¼ tsp sea salt
¼ tsp crushed garlic or 1 clove
Dash cayenne pepper
1 ½ tsp minced fresh dill or basil or ½ tsp dried
1 tsp minced onion

Ranch Dressing:
Blend:
1 cup raw cashews that have been soaked for one hour
¼ cup water
2 T lemon juice
½ tsp garlic powder
½ tsp onion powder
1 T chopped fresh basil
1 T chopped fresh dill
Sea salt to taste

Creamy Avocado Dressing:
Blend:
1 - 2 chopped avocados depending on the size
1 clove of garlic minced
Juice of one lemon
½ red pepper or cucumber chopped
Pinch of sea salt and a dash of pepper (add water to desired consistency)

Simple Tahini Dressing:
Blend:
¼ cup tahini
2 T olive or flax oil
1 T minced garlic
2 or 3 T lemon juice
1 T tamari
Pinch of sea salt and a dash of pepper (add a bit of water if too thick)

Spicy Tahini Dressing:
Blend:
1 cup raw tahini
1 cup olive oil
10 garlic cloves
2 tsp sea salt
2 cups filtered water
2 T cumin
½ cup lemon juice

Janet McKee Success Coach, Wellness Expert, Speaker and Author
CEO and Founder of SanaView
janet@sanaview.com
©SanaView 2018. All rights reserved.

Creamy Tahini Dressing:
Blend:
½ jar of raw tahini
½ cup lemon juice
¼ cup apple cider vinegar
½ cup olive oil
¼ cup water
¼ cup Nama Shoyu
A few dashes of Cayenne
Sea salt and pepper to taste
Fresh ginger
Powdered garlic
Honey or natural sweetener of choice
Fresh crushed garlic

Optional add ons:
Sun-dried tomatoes
Miso
Herbs
Cilantro
Basil

Creamy Zucchini Tahini Dressing:
Blend:
4 zucchini chopped (may want to peel first)
4 garlic cloves
2 tsp sea salt
1 T cumin
½ cup lemon juice
1 cup raw tahini

Basic Tahini Dressing:
Blend:
1/2 cup raw tahini
1/4 cup lemon juice
½ tsp crushed garlic
¼ tsp sea salt
¼ tsp cumin
Dash cayenne
1 T minced fresh parsley
Add 1/3 cup of water if needed to obtain desired consistency

Orange Tahini Dressing:
Blend:
2 T raw tahini
6 red peppers or 6 tomatoes juiced
2 whole peeled lemons or simply juiced
2 slices sweet onion juiced
¼ tsp sea salt

Spinach Salad with Pears and Pecans

This is one salad that everyone loves. I often choose this one to serve for a dinner party or to bring to someone's home when I am invited as a guest. Feel free to vary the nut or fruit that you use to round out this salad. I love to add pomegranate seeds in the fall.

Ingredients:
1 firm pear, cored and sliced
4 green onions, thinly sliced
1 tsp sea salt
4 T extra-virgin olive oil
2 T apple cider vinegar
1 lemon juiced
1 T raw honey or maple syrup (optionally add more pears for sweetness)
1 pound of spinach leaves
½ cup of chopped parsley and cilantro
1/3 cup chopped pecans
Fresh black pepper

Preparation:
Toss pear and green onions with sea salt, olive oil, vinegar, lemon juice, and honey or maple syrup. Allow to marinate for 5 to 10 minutes. Add spinach leaves, chopped herbs, and pecans, and gently toss with salad servers. Season with additional salt and black pepper if necessary and enjoy.

Servings: 4 - 6

Janet McKee Success Coach, Wellness Expert, Speaker and Author
CEO and Founder of SanaView
janet@sanaview.com
©SanaView 2018. All rights reserved.

Raw (Fresh) Kale Salad

My good friend from Long Island, NY made this recipe for me once while visiting and it has been one of my favorites ever since. It always surprises me how much my son loves this salad too. It is the perfect combination of light oil and lemon that nicely enhances the flavor of the kale. This salad is great with arugula too, without the need to massage.

Ingredients:
1 bunch of kale
1 tsp sea salt
1 cup of chopped tomatoes or sliced sweet red pepper
¼ cup hemp seeds
Handful of dulse
3 T lemon juice
3 T flax or hemp or olive oil
Optionally add pomegranate seeds for color and nutrition

Janet McKee Success Coach, Wellness Expert, Speaker and Author
CEO and Founder of SanaView
janet@sanaview.com
©SanaView 2018. All rights reserved.

Preparation:
Rinse the kale, strip the leaves from the tough stem and chop into bit sized pieces.
Add the sea salt, lemon and oil and massage into the kale until it softens.
Add the remaining ingredients and toss.

You may decide to add some other vegetables to this salad, such as chopped avocado, cucumber or sprouts.

Servings: 4

Creamy Broccoli Salad

Adapted from the book "The Cancer Survivor's Guide". All ages love this salad, as it is creamy and fun to eat with all of the flavorful and colorful ingredients.

Ingredients:
2 medium broccoli stalks
2 or 3 green onions, chopped
1/2 cup shredded carrots
1/2 cup golden raisins
1/4 cup dried cranberries
3 tablespoons dairy- and egg-free mayonnaise substitute
1/4 cup seasoned rice vinegar
1/4 teaspoon black pepper

Preparation:
Cut broccoli florets into bite-size pieces.
Peel stems and cut into bite-size pieces.
Transfer to a salad bowl and add green onions, carrots, raisins, and cranberries.
In a small bowl, mix together mayonnaise substitute, vinegar, sugar, and black pepper.
Pour over broccoli and toss to mix. Let stand about 30 minutes before serving to allow flavors to blend.

Servings: 4

Raw Italian Style Kale and Collard Greens Salad

Adapted from a recipe by Jackie Graff. This is a wonderful use of fresh herbs and greens.

Ingredients:
3 cloves of garlic
2 T fresh oregano
½ cup fresh basil
2 T fresh thyme
1 medium onion finely chopped
1 red bell pepper
3 cups of chopped tomatoes
½ cup pine nuts
2 lemons juiced
½ cup olive oil
2 tsp sea salt
1 bunch of kale
1 bunch of collard greens

Preparation:
Rinse and chop kale and collards into fine strips.
Blend pine nuts, lemon juice, olive oil and salt and pour this dressing over the greens and massage well. Allow the greens to marinate for one hour.

Place garlic, oregano, thyme and basil in a food processor and finely chop.
Chop onions, tomatoes, red pepper and place in a large bowl.
After the greens have marinated, blend all ingredients together in the bowl and serve.

Servings: 8

Janet's Asian Slaw

I created this recipe one day when a group of friends were coming over and I happened to have several heads of cabbage from the local farmer. Feel free to use any fresh vegetable you have on hand to make this as varied or interesting as you like.

Ingredients:

½ head of green cabbage shredded
½ head of red cabbage shredded (or just use a whole head of green cabbage)
3 T sesame oil
4 T umeboshi plum vinegar
2 cloves of garlic, minced
¼ cup of chopped cilantro
2 shredded carrots
2 T black sesame seeds
1 cucumber chopped into small cubes
2 stalks of celery chopped into very small pieces
2 small tomatoes or ½ of a red pepper chopped into small pieces.

Janet McKee Success Coach, Wellness Expert, Speaker and Author
CEO and Founder of SanaView
janet@sanaview.com
©SanaView 2018. All rights reserved.

Preparation:
Shred the cabbage and chop all the vegetables into small pieces.

Combine in a large bowl and add the oil, vinegar, minced garlic and cilantro.

Toss and serve.

Servings: 8 - 10

Wild Rice Cranberry and Pecan Salad

I adapted this from an incredibly delicious and satisfying salad from my dear friends and colleagues, Dr. Stan and Jayne Wetschler.

Ingredients:
1 cup wild rice, sprouted [soak wild rice in water in mason jars for 24 – 48 hours until the rice begins to soften and split open, rinse and drain]
½ cups pecans, chopped
¼ cup green onions
½ cup chopped green apples
½ cup cranberries (optional)
2 T flat parsley, finely chopped
¼ cup celery, finely chopped
½ cup red, green and yellow peppers [any combination or one alone]
½ cup pomegranate seeds (optional)

Janet McKee Success Coach, Wellness Expert, Speaker and Author
CEO and Founder of SanaView
janet@sanaview.com
©SanaView 2018. All rights reserved.

Dressing:
1 T lemon juice
2 T olive oil
Juice of one orange
1 T of orange zest
½ tsp salt and pepper to taste

Preparation:
Mix together all of the solid ingredients in bowl.
Mix the dressing in a separate bowl and stir into the salad.
Add salt and pepper to taste.
Refrigerate for several hours to allow the flavors to incorporate.

Servings: 4 - 6

Blended Salad (or raw soup)

Often when clients are suffering with digestive discomfort for any reason, a blended salad is a wonderful way to get healing and cooling fresh vegetables in the diet while offering the body a chance to heal. This concept, courtesy of Paul Nison, saved me many times when my illness was in a flared condition. Use this as a platform for creating your own unique and delicious version. Some would consider this a raw soup.

Ingredients:
1 cucumber
1 tomato
1 stalk of celery
Juice of 1 lemon
Handful of spinach and/or romaine or any green of choice (I even like a combination of parsley and basil)
1 avocado
Pinch of sea salt to taste

You may even decide to add 1 clove of fresh garlic, flax oil, and turmeric to their anti-inflammatory qualities!

Preparation:
Cut the ingredients into small pieces, remove any seeds if necessary, and blend in a blender.
You may actually find that you do not need to add any water.

Servings: 2 - 4

Greens with Pine Nuts and Raisins

This recipe is so incredibly easy and delicious; it should be part of everyone's collection of favorite dishes.

Ingredients:
Large bunch of greens such as spinach, kale, collards, or Swiss chard
1 – 2 T olive oil, sesame oil or coconut oil (or you can water sauté by using a small amount of water in place of your cooking oil)
2 T of pine nuts
2 T of raisins or currants
Sea salt to taste – optional

Preparation:
Sauté nuts and raisins in oil until raisins are slightly soft and nuts begin to brown gently.

Add greens and cook briefly until soft but still bright green.

Servings: 2 - 4

Greens with Tahini Sauce

For those who feel that some of the truly healthy greens are just a bit too bitter to enjoy, try this recipe, as the sauce is divine and will make all green leafy vegetables a joy to eat.

Ingredients:
Steamed greens of choice such as kale, collards, spinach, Swiss chard, bok choy etc.
1/3 cup tahini
2 T Nama Shoyu or Tamari (soy sauce of choice or Bragg's Liquid Aminos)
2 T Umeboshi Vinegar
½ bunch parsley, chopped
½ bunch scallions, chopped
Put in food processor and pulse
1 cup water or less (add while processor is blending, use less for thicker dressing)

Preparation:
Steam greens for a few minutes.
Blend all remaining ingredients in a food processor or blender adding the water at the end while the processor is running.
Pour the tahini sauce over the greens and serve.

This tahini dressing can be used as a salad dressing or as a dip or spread if made thicker by using less water.

Servings: 2 - 4

Garlicky Greens

This is the simplest way to have some cooked greens to serve with any dish or eat as a main course.

Ingredients:
1 bunch of greens of choice such as kale, collards, spinach, Swiss chard, bok choy etc.
2 cloves of garlic chopped
pinch of crushed red pepper flakes (optional)
sea salt and pepper to taste

Optionally, you may add any other chopped veggie. I love to add either sweet red pepper or tomatoes to give the dish some color.

Preparation:
Wash and chop the greens into small pieces, removing the stems if you like.

Heat the oil and garlic in a pan (along with the hot pepper if you choose).

Add the chopped greens and other veggies.
Sprinkle with salt and pepper.

Stir until lightly cooked or cover with a lid until wilted.
Do not overcook your greens!

Servings: 2 - 4

Garlic Ginger Bok Choy Over Rice

Years ago, I remember eating at a local Asian restaurant and was thrilled to see sautéed bok choy on the menu. It was yummy and garlicky and great served with steamed rice. My favorite is actually baby bok choy that we grow at our farm. Bok choy is a cruciferous vegetable, which means it is delicious immune boosting ammunition against disease.

Ingredients:
1 T olive oil
2 cloves of garlic
1 ½ T minced ginger
2 T pine nuts
6 cups of chopped bok choy
2 T low sodium Tamari (wheat free soy sauce)
salt and pepper to taste

Preparation:
Sauté olive oil, ginger, garlic and pine nuts in a pan over medium-low heat for one to two minutes.
Add the bok choy and continue to cook for about 5 minutes until slightly tender. Add the Tamari and salt and pepper and sauté for one minute more.
Serve over steamed rice or quinoa and enjoy.

Servings: 4

Janet McKee Success Coach, Wellness Expert, Speaker and Author
CEO and Founder of SanaView
janet@sanaview.com
©SanaView 2018. All rights reserved.

Steamed Winter Squash with Broccoli and Cauliflower

This dish is so simple you really don't need a recipe – but here it is anyway to remind you to combine these wonderful fall and winter veggies.

Ingredients:
1/2 Acorn Squash or winter squash of choice
1/2 head of broccoli
1/2 head of cauliflower
1 -2 cloves of chopped garlic
Flax or olive oil
Sea salt and fresh ground pepper to taste

Preparation:
Chop vegetables into bite size pieces. Steam squash in a pot with a bit of water.

Once the squash begins to get tender, add the remaining vegetables and garlic and steam until slightly tender. Remove from heat and add oil, salt, and pepper.

Servings: 6

Green Beans with Hazelnuts and Orange Zest

The warmed hazelnut flavored oil with orange zest adds a surprisingly perfect flavor to these standard vegetables. This is an impressive side dish to serve during the holidays as well.

Ingredients:
1 bag of fresh or frozen green beans
½ cup hazelnuts roughly chopped in half
Zest of 1 or 2 organic oranges
1 T olive oil
Sea salt and fresh ground pepper to taste

Preparation:
Steam green beans in a small bit of water until cooked but still lightly crisp.
Warm hazelnuts in oil in a skillet, add cooked green beans, salt and pepper and toss to coat.
Remove from heat and add orange zest and toss further and serve.

Servings: 6

Lemony Smashed Potatoes

Various chefs on The Cooking Channel were making versions of smashed potatoes. From watching them, I was inspired to create my own.

Ingredients:
1 small bag of baby red skin potatoes or other small potatoes
4 T olive oil
2 cloves of garlic chopped

Dressing:
3 T olive oil
Zest of 2 lemons
3 T lemon juice
3 T of chopped fresh herbs using mostly parsley with a bit of basil or sage or thyme or chives
Sea salt and fresh ground pepper to taste

Preparation:
Wash the potatoes and cook in a pot of boiling water until softened.
Drain and allow to cool briefly.
Smash each small potato with the palm of your hand or by using a wide spatula, on a cutting board.

Heat 2 T of oil in a large frying pan and add the garlic. After the garlic has lightly cooked, add the smashed potatoes until they line the bottom of the pan.

Cook the potatoes until they brown on the bottom. Flip the potatoes over with a spatula, add 2 more tablespoons of oil and cook until they are browned on the second side.

Season with a bit of salt and pepper.
Move the potatoes onto a plate and drizzle with the herb/lemon dressing.

Servings: 4

Creamy Cauliflower

This is a great side dish alternative to starchy potatoes and the health benefits of another cruciferous vegetable, like cauliflower, are outstanding.

Ingredients:
1 head of cauliflower chopped
1/2 cup of vegetable broth
4 cloves of garlic
2 T extra virgin olive oil
½ tsp salt
Fresh ground pepper to taste
2 T snipped fresh chives

Preparation:
Steam the cauliflower and garlic in the vegetable broth until soft.

Place the cooked cauliflower/garlic mixture and all of the remaining ingredients into a food processor or mixer, except the chives, and puree.

Pour into a serving bowl and top with the chives.

Servings: 6

Sweet Potato or Yam Casserole

I created this recipe for Thanksgiving dinner. I was never a fan of the typical sugary sweet potato casserole with maple syrup and marshmallows. It always seemed more like a dessert than a dinner side dish to me. So, I created my own version that is plenty sweet naturally, without added sugar.

Ingredients:
2 pounds of sweet potatoes or yams
2 T coconut oil
1/3 cup unsweetened coconut milk
1/8 tsp ground nutmeg
1 cup of pecans coarsely chopped
Salt and pepper to taste

Preparation:
Preheat your oven to 350°

Cook the sweet potatoes until soft by either baking whole in the oven and then removing the skin or peeling first and chopping and roasting in the oven or boiling them in water.

Place the cooked potatoes in a bowl and mash.

Use some of the coconut oil to grease the inside bottom and sides of a casserole dish.

Melt the remaining coconut oil and mix with the pecans.

Mix the other ingredients into the potatoes, except for the pecans.

Pour the potato mixture into the casserole dish, sprinkle the pecans on top and bake in a 350° oven for 40 minutes.

Servings: 6

Brussels Sprouts with Ginger

This was adapted from "The Anti-Cancer Cookbook" by Dr. Julia Greer. I never cared for Brussels sprouts until I tried this recipe and proceeded to eat the whole bowl!

Ingredients:
1 cup sliced almonds
2 pounds Brussels sprouts
2 T olive or sesame oil
2 slices of fresh ginger
3 T date sugar or lakanto
1 tsp sea salt
¼ - ½ cup water

Preparation:
Cook almonds in a dry skillet over medium heat for about 3 to 4 minutes until lightly toasted. Remove almonds from the skillet and set aside.

Remove any tough outer leaves from the Brussels sprouts, trim the ends and cut into quarters lengthwise.

Heat the oil in the skillet and add slices of ginger and cook for 1 – 2 minutes to flavor the oil. Remove ginger and discard.

Add the Brussels sprouts to the oil, toss to cover with flavored oil, and stir-fry for 2 minutes.
Add sugar and salt and stir-fry for another 2 minutes.
Then, add a bit of water to the pan and stir-fry for 1 to 2 minutes until the water cooks off.
Repeat this procedure, adding water a few more times until the Brussels sprouts are tender and lightly browned.

Add toasted almonds and stir well to combine.

Servings: 8 servings

Janet McKee Success Coach, Wellness Expert, Speaker and Author
CEO and Founder of SanaView
janet@sanaview.com
©SanaView 2018. All rights reserved.

PASTA AND PASTA ALTERNATIVES

Growing up in an Italian family meant pasta was a key part of filling our tummies with amazing food and our hearts with great love. Thus, as I learned to eat healthier, I wanted a way to continue to enjoy the amazing flavors of tomatoes and basil, garlic and oil along with the heart and soul fulfillment of good pasta.

Well, during my exploration into food and nutrition to heal the body, I was pleased to discover that yes; pasta can be part of a very healthy diet. As a matter of fact, the Mediterranean diet has been revered as one of the healthier diets from around the world and all people wanting to prevent or reverse serious illnesses can include pasta as part of a healing regimen.

If you need to avoid wheat and/or gluten for various health reasons, you are probably well aware of the wide variety of gluten-free pasta choices available today such as those made with brown rice, quinoa, buckwheat or a combination of other gluten-free flours. Another option to enjoy the flavors of a typical Italian dish while avoiding the flour altogether, is spaghetti squash or zucchini. Spaghetti squash is stringy just like an angel-hair pasta and raw zucchini can turn into long spaghetti like strands by placing it through a Spirooli or Spirulizer slicer.

Combine your "pasta" of choice with all of the amazing sauces and vegetables that you have grown to love. Remember, enjoying the food you eat is part of enjoying a happy and healthy life. Find a way that works for you and begin enjoying a satisfying and fulfilling life.

Now as my father would say – "MANGIA"!

Janet McKee Success Coach, Wellness Expert, Speaker and Author
CEO and Founder of SanaView
janet@sanaview.com
©SanaView 2018. All rights reserved.

Simple Spaghetti Squash

Spaghetti squash is the perfect food to include when you are craving the flavors of pasta but may want to take a break from the standard wheat alternatives.

Ingredients:

1 spaghetti squash – any size
Flavoring of choice such as:
Tomato sauce
Vegan Parmesan or nutritional yeast (optional)

Or

Flax oil or olive oil
Sea salt and pepper
Optionally add any herbs you love (like sage or basil)

Preparation:
Pre-heat your oven to 400 degrees.
Carefully cut the squash in half and then half again.
Scoop out the seeds.
Place cut side down in a roasting pan with a bit of water and roast for 1 hour or until soft.

Once the squash is finished cooking, scrape out the insides and add the flavoring of choice.

Season with salt and pepper and add a bit of vegan grated Parmesan if desired.

Servings: 4 - 6 depending on the size of the squash

Spaghetti Squash Primavera

This is a wonderful way to combine many great vegetables in a tasty and satisfying dish. You may choose to use any variety of fresh vegetables, such as snow peas or zucchini or summer squash etc. Try a variety of herbs as well.

Ingredients:
1 spaghetti squash – any size
½ head broccoli
½ head cauliflower
½ red bell pepper
½ green or yellow bell pepper
1 cup of tomato sauce of choice or fresh tomatoes
1 handful of chopped leafy greens such as kale, collard greens or spinach
1 - 2 cloves of garlic
2 - 3 T olive oil
Dash red pepper flakes
Sea salt and black pepper to taste
Grated vegan Parmesan or nutritional yeast (optional)

Preparation:
Pre-heat your oven to 400 degrees.
Carefully cut the squash in half and then half again. Scoop out the seeds. Place cut side down in a roasting pan with a bit of water and roast for 1 hour or until soft.

While the squash is cooking, sauté the garlic and crushed red pepper in olive oil. Cut the broccoli and cauliflower into small bit size pieces and add them to the pan. Cut the peppers into thin 1 inch strips and add them to the pan. If using a tougher green, such as kale and collards, add to the other vegetables early enough to give them time to cook. If using a softer green such as spinach, add this toward the end of the cooking as they only need to heat through.

Add the tomatoes or sauce for added flavor and color.
Once the squash is finished cooking, scrape out the insides and add to the vegetables.
Season with salt and pepper and add a bit of grated vegan Parmesan if desired.

Servings: 4 - 6 depending on the size of the squash

Janet McKee Success Coach, Wellness Expert, Speaker and Author
CEO and Founder of SanaView
janet@sanaview.com
©SanaView 2018. All rights reserved.

Spring Pasta

This recipe was adapted from Martha Stewart Living. Again, this is one of my family's favorites.

Ingredients:
2 T olive oil
1 bag of frozen or fresh peas
6 spring onions thinly sliced
¼ cup chopped fresh parsley
2 T of fresh chopped sage
2 T of fresh chopped chives
1 clove of garlic finely chopped
Sea salt
1 bunch of spinach or arugula leaves
1 pound of linguine pasta or Japanese udon noodles
Vegan Parmesan or nutritional yeast to taste
Freshly ground pepper to taste

Preparation:
Heat one tablespoon of olive oil in a pan. Add peas and sea salt and cook covered for a few minutes until tender. Remove to a small bowl.

Heat another tablespoon of oil in the same pan. Add the spring onions, parsley, sage, chives and garlic. Once these ingredients have softened slightly, add the peas, additional salt and 1 tablespoon of water back to the pan. Cook covered for a few minutes more until the onions are bright green. Toss in the spinach or arugula and set aside.

Cook the pasta according to the package directions. Drain the pasta and add to the pea and herb mixture and toss. Sprinkle with vegan cheese or nutritional yeast and drizzle with additional olive oil and sprinkle more fresh parsley if necessary.

Servings: 4 - 6

Pasta with Kale, Tomatoes and Olives

As part of my health practice, I represent the Physician's Committee for Responsible Medicine and for them, I teach Food for Life classes. This recipe I adapted from The Cancer Survivor's Guide by Dr. Neal Barnard and Jennifer Reilly, which is the book we use for that class.

Ingredients:

1/2 cup vegetable broth or water
2 cloves of garlic chopped
2 medium onions diced
2 heads of kale chopped
6 cups of chopped fresh tomatoes (or jarred crushed or chopped tomatoes) *
1 cup pitted Kalamata olives
2 T chopped fresh parsley
16 ounces of pasta (this works well with penne or a similar shape, try whole wheat, quinoa, or brown rice pasta)
½ cup vegan Parmesan or nutritional yeast

*the lining of the cans for canned tomatoes have been sprayed with BPA, which is why I suggest using fresh or jarred tomatoes.

Preparation:

Cook pasta in salted boiling water until slightly under cooked or al dente.

While pasta is cooking, sauté garlic and onion in the vegetable broth over medium heat until they begin to soften. Add the kale and tomatoes and heat through without over cooking. The kale should still be bright green. Add olives and parsley and heat through.

Add the cooked pasta to the vegetables and stir to combine the flavors. Sprinkle with vegan Parmesan or nutritional yeast and serve.

Servings: 8

Pasta with Butternut Squash, Sage and Greens

Right when I was inundated with butternut squash from our farm, I stumbled up this wonderful idea that I adapted from Martha Stewart Living to be healthier but equally as delicious. What was most interesting to me is that I recently learned from a client of mine that she loves to save and roast the squash seeds. I did some research and discovered that the seeds are a great source of protein and healthy fats. It is amazing that this recipe includes the squash seeds too.

Ingredients:

1 lb of pasta of choice (consider brown rice or quinoa pasta for gluten free alternatives)
2 T extra virgin olive oil
1 small butternut squash (about 4 cups)
3 T coconut oil
¼ C packed fresh sage leaves
Salt and pepper to taste
Optionally add a handful of winter greens such as kale, spinach or tatsoi

Janet McKee Success Coach, Wellness Expert, Speaker and Author
CEO and Founder of SanaView
janet@sanaview.com
©SanaView 2018. All rights reserved.

Preparation:
Remove the ends of the butternut squash and cut it in half.
Remove the seeds and pulp and reserve
Cut the remaining butternut squash into small bite-sized pieces.
Cook the pasta in salted boiling water until al dente. Save ½ cup of the pasta cooking water.

While the pasta is cooking, heat the olive oil in a saucepan and sauté the squash, pulp and seeds until the seeds turn golden, which will take about 10minutes.
Season the pulp and seeds with salt and place on a plate to reserve.
Sauté the sage leaves in the coconut oil in the same saucepan until crisp.
Move to a plate to reserve.

Place the butternut squash chunks in the same pan and cook covered for about 10 minutes until soft. Season with salt and pepper.
Add the cooked pasta, the reserved pasta water and some winter greens to the pan with the butternut squash and cook for a few minutes until thickened.
Add the squash seeds and pulp and sage to the pasta and serve.

Servings: 4 - 6

Raw Zucchini Pasta

Yes, raw foodists can have pasta too. This is fun as a vegetable side dish for others as well. You will need either a spiralizer or Spirooli slicer to easily turn the zucchini into noodles.

Ingredients:

6 – 8 Spiralized Zucchini – turns the zucchini into long noodle like strips.

Use one of the following sauce alternatives for the zucchini noodles:

Tomato Sauce	No Sauce	Pesto Sauce	Alfredo Sauce
Fresh tomatoes	Sliced tomatoes	2 cups of fresh basil	2 ½ cups of nuts (pine, cashew, or macadamia)
Handful of soaked sun-dried tomatoes	Chopped basil	2 T pine nuts	1 tsp. of fresh herbs
Fresh thyme, oregano, basil and parsley	Olive oil	1 clove of garlic	1-2 cloves of garlic
Sea salt	Sea salt	½ cup of extra virgin olive oil	2 T lemon juice
Avocado (optional)	Minced garlic	Sea salt	1-2 cups of water to desired consistency
	Pine nuts or walnuts	2 T grated Romano cheese (optional)	Salt and pepper to taste

Preparation:
Run the zucchini through a slicer to create long thin noodle shapes. You may put some sea salt on the noodles and let it sit a while to soften like cooked pasta. Add the sauce of choice above and serve. Amazing!

Servings: 4

Janet McKee Success Coach, Wellness Expert, Speaker and Author
CEO and Founder of SanaView
janet@sanaview.com
©SanaView 2018. All rights reserved.

Simple Pasta with Oil and Garlic
This is straight from the kitchen of my mom and grandmother. This is a simple and delicious Italian dish.

Ingredients:
1 pound of pasta (consider whole grain, quinoa, brown rice or Asian udon or soba noodles)
½ cup extra virgin olive oil
2 cloves of garlic
¼ - ½ tsp crushed chilies
1T finely chopped parsley
Sea salt

Optionally add in: (just cook in the oil and garlic until done):
Any veggie you choose – this is amazing with broccoli florets
or
Combination of red kidney or adzuki beans and spinach

Preparation:
Cook the pasta according to the package directions.
As the pasta is cooking, sauté the garlic and chilies in oil on low heat being careful not to burn the garlic.
Add some parsley and salt and set aside.

Once the pasta is slightly underdone, or al dente, drain the pasta and add it to the garlic and oil mixture.

Servings: 6

Simple Freshly Cooked Tomato Sauce

For a truly authentic Italian taste, be sure to try this late in the summer when you are inundated with fresh tomatoes. This tastes exactly how my grandmother used to make a quick bowl of pasta. Don't hesitate to try some of the gluten free quinoa or brown rice pastas as an alternative to wheat.

Ingredients:

2 ½ cups of chopped fresh tomatoes in season
3 cloves of garlic finely chopped
4 T extra virgin olive oil
2 T fresh basil finely chopped
Salt and pepper to taste
1 pound of dried pasta

Preparation:
Cook the pasta according to the package directions.

As the pasta is cooking, sauté the garlic in oil on low heat, being careful not to burn the garlic.
Add the chopped tomatoes and season with salt and pepper.
Cook for just a few minutes to heat through, and add the chopped basil at the last minute before removing from heat.

Once the pasta is slightly underdone, or al dente, drain the pasta and add it to the tomato sauce and stir to combine.

Servings: 6

Fall Harvest Pasta

One September day when my farm manager and I were harvesting produce for the Mother Earth News Fair at Seven Springs Mountain Resort, we got very hungry so we took a small amount of everything we were harvesting and created this truly awesome pasta dish.

Ingredients:

4 T olive oil or vegetable broth
3 cloves of garlic
A variety of small hot peppers chopped such as cayenne, jalapeno or shishito (optional)
1 sweet pepper of choice
1 large or 2 small eggplants of any variety sliced
1 zucchini or yellow squash sliced
A few leaves of kale ripped from the stem and chopped
1 cup of fresh chopped tomatoes
salt and pepper to taste

Janet McKee Success Coach, Wellness Expert, Speaker and Author
CEO and Founder of SanaView
janet@sanaview.com
©SanaView 2018. All rights reserved.

Preparation:
Sauté garlic and peppers in oil or broth until softened.
Add the eggplant and zucchini to the pan and cook until softened and golden brown.
Add torn kale and chopped tomatoes and heat through.
Add salt and pepper throughout cooking process.

Add the vegetable mixture to a pound a freshly cooked pasta and enjoy!

Servings: 4

WHOLE GRAIN COMFORTS AND HEARTY MAIN DISHES

All of the other foods discussed so far can be combined to make wonderfully delicious and beautiful meals. For example, enjoy soup or pasta and salad or a stew and vegetable side dish etc. There are, however, a few additional recipes to help complete the meals for a family for the week.

Including whole grain side dishes with any other recipe is a wonderful addition. I particularly love quinoa and brown rice but sometimes make millet too. Like any grain, they are very easy to cook. It is always one cup of grain to two cups water, bring the pot to a boil and turn down to simmer, leaving the lid on. The only difference is the length of time you cook each grain. So, for brown rice, it is 50 minutes, for millet it is 30 minutes, and for quinoa, 15 minutes. I love these grains because they are gluten free and absolutely delicious.

I use any of these whole grains as a base for any soup or stew. This makes the meal heartier and satisfying. Sometimes, I just cook millet and serve it with tomato sauce and veggies just like any pasta. This is a great alternative to pasta in addition to all those mentioned in the previous section. And of course, you can add vegetables and lentils too – this is very yummy.

I use tempeh often too as this is a very healthy meat-like ingredient. It is a complete protein but because the soybeans are fermented, it makes them very easy to digest. You can do anything with tempeh that you would consider doing with meat such as grill, include in a stir-fry, or even put on a sandwich. Have fun learning how to use some of these foods if they are new to you. Searching the Internet for ideas is very inspiring.

Orange and Walnut Quinoa
Adapted from the Institute for Integrative Nutrition 2007

Ingredients:
1 cup quinoa
The zest of 2 navel oranges
½ cups chopped toasted walnuts
2 cups vegetable broth
2 T flat leaf parsley

Preparation:
Rinse quinoa in a fine mesh strainer.
Add the broth and quinoa, and bring to a boil.
Cover and lower heat to low, cooling for 12 minutes
Remove from heat and let stand for 5 minutes
Fluff with a fork and toss in orange zest, parsley and toasted walnuts

Servings: 4

Janet's Yummy Rice

I serve this often to large crowds because everyone loves this "yummy" rice.

Ingredients:
2 cups rice (I recommend any type of brown rice)
4 cups water
2 large vegetable bouillon cubes
(or use 4 cups of vegetable broth instead of water/bouillon combination)
Sea salt if needed
1 large leek, cut in half and then sliced and rinsed
2 T of olive oil or coconut oil
½ bunch of fresh parsley
½ bag of fresh or frozen peas

Preparation:
Place rice in water or broth in a saucepan. Bring to a boil. Reduce heat and simmer for recommended length of time to cook the rice (50 minutes for brown rice).

As the rice is cooking, sauté the leeks in oil for a few minutes until tender. Cook the peas in a separate pot in ¼ cup of water until tender also. Add leeks, peas, and chopped parsley to the rice, when finished, and serve.

Servings: 6

Janet's Mediterranean Rice Salad

I created this one summer day when we were having friends and neighbors over for a picnic.

Ingredients:
2 cups rice (I recommend any type of brown or basmati rice)
4 cups vegetable broth
1 large cucumber
¼ cup soaked chopped sun-dried tomatoes
½ cup of fresh chopped basil
¼ - ½ cup of fresh parsley chopped
¼ - ½ cup of chopped Kalamata olives

Dressing:
½ cup olive oil
Juice and zest of 1 large lemon (or more to desired taste)
1 tsp salt
½ tsp pepper

Preparation:
Place rice in broth in a saucepan. Bring to a boil. Reduce heat and simmer for recommended length of time to cook the rice (50 minutes for brown rice).

While the rice is cooking, chop the cucumbers, tomatoes, basil, parsley and olives and add to a large salad bowl.
In a separate bowl or jar, whisk together the dressing ingredients.

Once the rice is done cooking, add the cooked rice to the salad bowl with veggies. Add the dressing on top and toss. Be prepared to add more lemon, salt and pepper to taste as desired.

Servings: 8 - 10

Janet McKee Success Coach, Wellness Expert, Speaker and Author
CEO and Founder of SanaView
janet@sanaview.com
©SanaView 2018. All rights reserved.

Saffron Rice with Pine Nuts and Asparagus

This is a recipe from a workshop I taught on depression. Saffron has been found to help combat depression.

Ingredients:
2 cups rice
4 cups vegetable broth
a pinch of saffron
a small bunch of asparagus
2 T olive oil
salt and pepper to taste
2 T pine nuts
fresh parsley

Preparation:
Cook the rice in the broth with the saffron as directed.
In a pan, sauté asparagus and pine nuts in olive oil and season with salt and pepper.
Combine the asparagus and pine nuts to the rice once it is done cooking.
Garnish the rice with fresh parsley and enjoy.

Servings: 4-6

Risotto with Butternut Squash and Spinach

My son found this recipe on the food network but it was loaded with heavy cheeses and fatty chicken broth. He made some healthy changes by eliminating the cheese and using vegetable broth and it was so delicious, it became one of our favorite mid-winter dishes when butternut squash is still available and spinach is growing in our greenhouse.

Ingredients:
2 T of coconut oil or olive oil
1 handful of fresh sage leaves
1 onion chopped
3 cloves of garlic, minced
2 cups of peeled and chopped butternut squash
1 ½ cups of Arborio rice
¼ cup of dry white wine (optional)
4 cups of vegetable broth
2 cups of fresh spinach
sea salt and fresh ground pepper to taste

Janet McKee Success Coach, Wellness Expert, Speaker and Author
CEO and Founder of SanaView
janet@sanaview.com
©SanaView 2018. All rights reserved.

Preparation:

Heat the vegetable broth in a separate saucepan.

Sauté the sage, onion and garlic for about 1 minute in oil until it softens or turns lightly brown.

Add the butternut squash and 1 tsp of salt and cook for about 5 minutes until the squash begins to soften.

Add the rice and about 1 cup of broth and stir often until the broth absorbs.

Continue to add more broth and the wine, one cup at a time, allowing each cup to absorb into the rice and squash while stirring often.

As you finish using the remaining broth and wine, the rice should be done cooking.

Add the spinach and stir in until the spinach softens.

Add additional salt and pepper as needed, remove from the heat and enjoy.

Servings: 4

Tempeh Broccoli Sauté

This recipe is from the book, "The Cancer Survivor's Guide".
This is a delicious way to introduce tempeh, which is a wonderful source of protein from fermented soybeans.

Ingredients:
1 10-ounce package of tempeh
¼ cup vegetable broth
2 bunches of broccoli chopped (or 16 ounces each of frozen broccoli florets)
1 small onion, diced
1 red bell pepper, diced
1 T minced garlic
1 T peeled and minced ginger (or 1 tsp of ground ginger)
1 T soy sauce
2 C cooked brown rice, millet or quinoa for serving

Preparation:
Cut the tempeh into ½ inch cubes and steam in some of the vegetable broth or water for 10 minutes in a large wok or skillet.

Add the broccoli, onion, bell pepper, garlic and ginger. Cook and stir over medium-high heat until the tempeh is lightly browned and the vegetables are tender crisp.

Add the soy sauce just before serving.
Serve over the cooked grains and enjoy!

Servings: 4

Sautéed Asian Tempeh

This is one of my favorite ways to serve tempeh. The combination of sweetness from the apples with the contrasting flavors of vinegar and tamari is wonderful.

Ingredients:
1 block of tempeh cut into sections
½ cup of fresh apple juice
1 T of brown rice vinegar
1 ½ T low sodium tamari or soy sauce
2 – 3 T sesame oil

Preparation:
Sauté each piece of tempeh in sesame oil for 5 minutes until golden brown on both sides.
Add apple juice, brown rice vinegar and soy sauce and cook for approximately 15 to 20 minutes or until all the liquid has evaporated.

Servings: 8

Tempeh Tacos

Tempeh can be used as a meat alternative for any dish. This is a fun way to use this healthful food.

Ingredients:
2 Tbsp. olive oil
1 large onion, chopped
12 oz. plain tempeh, crumbled into large pieces
1 Tbsp. tamari
1 tsp. ground cumin
1 dozen corn tortillas (approximately), wrapped in foil
1/2 - 1 cup coarsely chopped fresh cilantro
2 cups crisp lettuce (e.g., romaine), washed and shredded

Preparation:
In a large skillet, heat the oil and sauté the onion over medium-high heat, stirring often, for about 5 minutes, or until onion is browned around the edges and fragrant.

Add tempeh, tamari, and cumin; reduce heat to medium and stir until tempeh is slightly browned, about 3 minutes.

Turn off heat, adjust seasonings to taste, and cover to keep warm.

Meanwhile, warm tortillas in a 350°F oven until they are soft and pliable.
Fold each tortilla in half, and spoon in the tempeh mixture; top with cilantro, lettuce, and salsa, and serve immediately.

Servings: 4 - 6

Raw Walnut Tacos

This recipe was shared with me from a good friend and colleague, Amy Bencho. She adapted this recipe that she discovered while learning about raw foods at Halleluiah Acres.

Ingredients:
1 ½ cups of raw walnuts
1 ½ tsp ground cumin
¾ tsp ground coriander
2 T of Nama Shoyu or Tamari
3 to 4 small or medium collard green, romaine or cabbage leaves
1 cup of shredded lettuce
Top with fresh tomato salsa (see earlier recipe) and/or guacamole (see earlier recipe) or simply chopped avocado

Preparation:
Grind walnuts in a food processor into a "meaty" consistency.
In a small bowl, combine the walnuts, cumin, and coriander and mix well.
Add the Nama Shoyu and mix.

Spread approximately 1/3 cup of the walnut mixture along the center stem of each leaf, and then add a layer of shredded lettuce.

Top with salsa and guacamole and serve.

Servings: 4

Spicy Garbanzo Burgers

This recipe is from the book, "The Cancer Survivor's Guide" and is one of our favorites.

Ingredients:

2 T raw sesame seeds
1 small onion
1 small carrot
1 stalk of celery
1 clove of garlic
1 can of garbanzo beans (chick peas) rinsed and drained
    (or 1 ½ cups cooked)
½ cup cooked brown rice
1 T soy sauce or tamari
1 ½ tsp curry powder
1 tsp ground cumin
½ tsp salt
½ tsp ground coriander or cardamom
1/8 tsp cayenne
¼ cup potato flour

Janet McKee Success Coach, Wellness Expert, Speaker and Author
CEO and Founder of SanaView
janet@sanaview.com
©SanaView 2018. All rights reserved.

Preparation:
Cook the sesame seeds in a dry skillet until they become fragrant or leave them raw. Place them in a spice grinder or food processor and grind. Place them in a mixing bowl.

Chop the onion, carrot, celery, garlic, and beans in a food processor until it appears like a "ground meat" mixture, leaving some small chunks.

Place the vegetable and bean mixture in the bowl with the sesame seeds and add the remaining spices.

Add enough potato flour to form a somewhat dryer mixture.

Form the mixture into patties and cook in a skillet over medium heat on each side until lightly browned and heated through. Serve like any burger with your favorite condiments.

Servings: 6 burgers

Raw and Dehydrated Soft Corn Tortillas

These are so delicious; you do not need to be a raw foodist to love these!

Ingredients:
3 cups fresh organic corn (about 4 ears) or one bag of frozen corn thawed
1 lime juiced
1 ½ red bell peppers
¾ cup ground flax seed
1 T chili powder
1 ½ tsp sea salt
1 T nutritional yeast
2 tsp ground cumin

Preparation:
Mix all of the ingredients, except the flax seed, in a food processor until a smooth batter is formed. Place in a bowl and mix in the ground flax seed by hand.

Spread the mixture onto dehydrator sheets lined with Teflex to about a 1/8-inch thickness. Dehydrate for one hour at 120 degrees. Turn the dehydrator down to 115 degrees and dehydrate for about 4 hours.

Carefully turn the dehydrator sheet upside down onto the countertop and pull the Teflex sheet off of the back of the tortilla shells, exposing the moist side. Place back into the dehydrator with the moist side up and continue to dehydrate for another 2 – 3 hours. Be sure to check the tortillas to make sure they are dry but still bendable. Be careful not to over dehydrate or they will be too brittle to bend into taco shells. Remove the sheets from the dehydrator and cut into 4-inch rounds using a saucer as a guide. Save the scraps for snacking or for topping soups and salads.

Serve filled with your favorite nut pate, salsa and guacamole.
You can keep the tortilla shells in the freezer for up to 2 months.

Servings: 8 tortillas

Black Bean and Corn Enchiladas

I created this with simple ingredients as an alternative to meat filled dishes.

Ingredients:
1 15oz can of black beans (or 1 cup dried and cooked)
½ bag of frozen corn (or 1 cup of fresh)
1 small zucchini chopped into small bite-size pieces
1 red pepper chopped into small bite-size pieces
6 tortillas
2 cloves garlic
2 T olive oil
1 cup rice or soy cheese, Monterey jack and/or cheddar flavors
2 - 3 fresh tomatoes chopped
½ cup chopped cilantro
Sea salt
Fresh ground black pepper
1 T cayenne (or to taste)
2 T ground cumin (or to taste)

Preparation:
Cook corn and zucchini together and set aside. Sauté the garlic in 1 tablespoon of olive oil until it is tender. Add red pepper and black beans and cook until tender. Mix in corn and zucchini. Add salt, cayenne and cumin. Cook for a few minutes to allow flavors to blend. Add fresh ground black pepper.

Pre-heat your oven to 350 degrees.

Place filling and cheese in each tortilla shell. Roll or fold over the shell and top with additional cheese. Drizzle with the remaining olive oil. Place in the oven for about 15 minutes until the cheese melts and the tortillas begin to brown.
Top the enchiladas with chopped tomato and chopped cilantro. Serve with guacamole and chopped lettuce.

Servings: 4

Janet McKee Success Coach, Wellness Expert, Speaker and Author
CEO and Founder of SanaView
janet@sanaview.com
©SanaView 2018. All rights reserved.

TRULY HEALTHY DECADENT DESSERTS

The Italians say a day without wine is like a day without sunshine. Well, I say that about dessert. Including something sweet and decadent and sometimes creamy at times throughout the day certainly adds to my happiness. Well, knowing that the fabulous dessert I am eating also happens to be good for me is certainly an amazing feeling.

Do not deprive yourself of the wonderful sweet taste that some foods offer. Do, however, choose sweet treats that support great health and vitality. It is actually very simple and the following pages give you ideas on how to make this possible.

I like to build upon the natural sweet taste of fruit in making a decision to have dessert. Fruit has so many health benefits such as fiber, nutrients and antioxidants and the fact that it tastes great is quite a bonus. I try not to use too many simple sugars. Yes, honey, maple syrup, brown rice syrup and agave nectar are natural sweeteners, however, they are still simple sugars and I like to include them only when necessary.

You will see in the following recipes that I rarely use simple sugars and instead rely on the natural sweetness of fruits or I use some natural, zero calorie, zero glycemic sweeteners such as stevia, Organic Zero or Lakanto. Unlike stevia, Organic Zero and Lakanto are true one-for-one natural sugar alternative so they can be used in any dessert recipe you already have. For example, I made a strawberry rhubarb pie for my family by adding Lakanto to the fruit and putting it all in a wonderful whole wheat crust. My family enjoyed the pie immensely and I felt good knowing that they were eating healthy foods with no added simple sugars.

Yes, truly healthy desserts as part of a truly healthy diet - now that is living well!

Janet McKee Success Coach, Wellness Expert, Speaker and Author
CEO and Founder of SanaView
janet@sanaview.com
©SanaView 2018. All rights reserved.

Mayan Hot Chocolate

This is an excerpt from the Mayan Celebration book of recipes created by Janet McKee to raise money for the Council of Thirteen Indigenous Grandmothers.

Even though the Aztecs valued cacao beans so greatly, they used the little dark beans as money, it was the Mayans who developed this bean into a food. Their original hot chocolate was made with hot water as they did not have cows!! It was made with chocolate, hot water, honey and a dash of salt. At home, I make my hot chocolate with raw organic chocolate powder and hot water (like tea), then I add stevia. Our modern culture, however, enjoys a richer version made with milk... Dark chocolate has been found to have several health benefits when used in moderation and not combined with dairy. By using one of the wonderful milk alternatives available, this drink can remain a healthful treat.

Janet McKee Success Coach, Wellness Expert, Speaker and Author
CEO and Founder of SanaView
janet@sanaview.com
©SanaView 2018. All rights reserved.

Traditional Version:
Ingredients:
5 cups non-dairy milk (vanilla almond milk works well also)
1 vanilla bean (or real vanilla extract)
2 cinnamon sticks
8 ounces of bittersweet chocolate
2 T of preferred sweetener such as sugar, honey, agave, stevia, Organic Zero or Lakanto (optional)
A pinch of cayenne pepper

Preparation:
In a saucepan, combine milk, vanilla bean and cinnamon sticks. Heat the mixture over medium flame until bubbles appear around the edge. Add chocolate and a sweetener, if you prefer to use one. Reduce heat to low. Whisk occasionally until chocolate has melted. Turn off heat and stir in a pinch of cayenne pepper to desired taste.

Janet's Healthier Metabolism Raising Version:
Use hot water instead of milk, then add vanilla, cinnamon stick, cocoa or raw cacao powder, stevia and cayenne.

Servings: 4 - 6

Nut Milk

I am repeating a variation of these from the breakfast/smoothie section of the book because the cherry-chocolate nut milk drink is an amazing dessert type treat!

Ingredients:
1 cup of fresh raw almonds soaked in water for at least 8 hours or 1 cup of Brazil nuts or cashews soaked for at least 15 minutes or use hemp seeds that do not need to be soaked and rinsed
5 cups fresh spring or filtered water (less water for thicker consistency)
Dash of sea salt
1 tsp alcohol free vanilla extract or whole vanilla bean

Preparation:
Soak the almonds in water for 8 – 12 hours or Brazil nuts for at least 15 minutes. Drain and rinse the soaked nuts. Add the nuts to a blender with the water, sea salt and vanilla. Blend until the nuts are fully processed. Optionally, you may pour the milk through a nut milk bag to remove any of the nut solids.

Servings: 5

Recipe suggestion:
Cherry Chocolate Milk

One of my favorite uses of nut milk is this absolutely yummy treat that satisfies any sweet or chocolate craving. I take half of the nut milk from the recipe above, I add an entire bag of frozen organic cherries and 1 – 2 tablespoons of raw cacao powder and blend.

Enjoy!!!!

"*Milk*" Shakes

My son and I love to enjoy a wonderful yummy but healthy "milk" shake when he comes home from school. It's times like these we know that life is good!!!

Ingredients:
2 cups of nut milk or any non-dairy milk of choice
2 frozen bananas
Optionally, for a more gourmet flavor you may add:
Dash of sea salt
1 tsp alcohol free vanilla extract

Then select the flavor for your "milk" shake by choosing one of the following:

For a chocolate milk shake:
2 T Raw cacao powder or a good organic cocoa powder (no sugar or dairy added)

For a strawberry milk shake:
1 small bag of frozen strawberries or fresh strawberries

Janet McKee Success Coach, Wellness Expert, Speaker and Author
CEO and Founder of SanaView
janet@sanaview.com
©SanaView 2018. All rights reserved.

For a peach milk shake:
1 small bag of frozen peaches or 2 fresh peaches in season

For a blueberry milk shake:
1 small bag of frozen blueberries or 1 pint of fresh

For a raspberry milk shake:
1 small bag of frozen raspberries or 1 pint fresh

For my favorite cherry chocolate milk:
Add one small bag of frozen cherries and 1 heaping T of cocoa powder

I think you get the idea!

Preparation:
Place all of the ingredients in a blender and blend until smooth. Then enjoy!!

Servings: 2 - 3

Berry Dessert Smoothie

This recipe is from the book, "The Cancer Survivor's Guide".
This is a double size recipe for the lecture attendees.
You can halve all of the ingredients to make enough for 1 - 2 people.

Ingredients:
2 - 3 cups of nut milk or any non-dairy milk
2 cups of frozen bananas
2 cups of either frozen strawberries or blueberries
4 T apple juice concentrate
1 tsp vanilla extract

Preparation:
Place all in a blender and enjoy!

Servings: 4 - 6

Janet McKee Success Coach, Wellness Expert, Speaker and Author
CEO and Founder of SanaView
janet@sanaview.com
©SanaView 2018. All rights reserved.

Soft Serve "Ice Cream" Frozen Dessert

I served this to my son for breakfast once and every boy in the neighborhood wanted to sleep over my house that night! This is perfectly healthy and perfectly delicious. Consider adding crushed walnuts or pecans on top for added texture, flavor, and nutritional content.

Ingredients:
2 ripe frozen bananas
1 bag of frozen fruit such as strawberries, blue berries, raspberries, peaches or mangoes

Preparation:
Cut the frozen bananas into chunks. Place one banana chunk at a time through a juicer with one bunch of frozen fruit of choice. This will come out of the juicer tasting like soft serve ice cream in the flavor of the fruit you choose.

If you don't have a juicer, do it in the blender!
Add 1/4 cup of non-dairy milk so that the above ingredients blend. A high-powered blender like the Vitamix works best. You may need to use a tamper to help the blender combine the ingredients into an ice cream consistency.

Servings: 2 - 4

Chocolate Banana Frozen Dessert

With no added fat or sugar, this is an amazing way to enjoy a perfectly healthy chocolate decadent treat.

Ingredients:
4 ripe bananas
2 T unsweetened cocoa powder or raw cacao powder
1 tsp pure vanilla extract

Preparation:
Place everything in a food processor or blender and blend until smooth. You may want to add a bit of water to help it blend. Place in individual dessert bowls and freeze until just frozen. Serve with thawed frozen or fresh raspberries, strawberries or cherries for a rich and colorful treat.

Servings: 2 - 4

Janet McKee Success Coach, Wellness Expert, Speaker and Author
CEO and Founder of SanaView
janet@sanaview.com
©SanaView 2018. All rights reserved.

Sugar Free Chocolate Mousse

I created this for my clients who could not have any sugar or even sweet fruit. It ended up being a favorite for all of my clients and class attendees.

Ingredients:
1 avocado
½ cup almond milk, rice milk or any non-dairy milk
1/3 cup of soaked dates or Organic Zero or Lakanto natural sweetener
½ cup raw cacao powder

Preparation:
If using sweeteners, place the milk and sweetener in a saucepot and warm on the stove until the sugar is melted.
Set aside to cool.
If using dates, soak the dates in water for at least 15 minutes, remove from the water and remove the pits. Blend with the milk in a high-speed blender.
Place avocado and cacao powder in a food processor and add the sweetened milk and blend until smooth. Enjoy!!

Servings: 4

Janet McKee Success Coach, Wellness Expert, Speaker and Author
CEO and Founder of SanaView
janet@sanaview.com
©SanaView 2018. All rights reserved.

Berries with Cashew Whipped Cream

I created this dessert one summer when I was craving fresh berries with whipped cream. Well, to avoid the high fat dairy and processed sugar (or worse yet, the processed vegetable oils and high fructose corn syrup and chemicals of non-dairy whipped topping), I decided to create a healthy yet satisfying alternative. You are sure to love this one!

Ingredients:
1 cup of raw cashews or macadamia nuts soaked in water for at least one hour
1/3 cup of dates soaked in water
¼ cup of date soaking water
2 tsp vanilla

Preparation:
Rinse and drain the nuts after soaking
Put all of the ingredients into a high-speed blender and blend into a whipped cream consistency.
Dollop over a bowl of fresh berries and enjoy

Servings: 4 - 6

Janet McKee Success Coach, Wellness Expert, Speaker and Author
CEO and Founder of SanaView
janet@sanaview.com
©SanaView 2018. All rights reserved.

Low Sugar Apple Crisp

I created this recipe for all clients wanting to reduce sugar intake to support their health and well-being. This is especially helpful for people with diabetes, pre-diabetes or candida (yeast imbalance).

Ingredients:
1.5 pounds of granny smith apples
1 T lemon juice
¼ cup Organic Zero or Lakanto
½ tsp ground cinnamon
¼ tsp nutmeg
1/3 cup of almonds for the almond flour (see note below)
2 T coconut oil
½ cup chopped almonds

Preparation:
Wash and chop the apples and remove the core. Place the chopped apples in a bowl and add the lemon juice and toss.

In a separate bowl, mix sweetener, cinnamon, and nutmeg together. Sprinkle half of this mixture over the apples and toss to coat, save the rest to sprinkle on top before baking.

Place 1/3 cup of fresh raw almonds in a food processor and process into an almond flour.
Cut in the coconut oil with the almond flour, the remaining sugar mixture and the chopped almonds.

Sprinkle the almond flour sugar mixture over the apples and bake in a roasting pan at 375 degrees for about 30 minutes.

Servings: 4 - 6

Janet McKee Success Coach, Wellness Expert, Speaker and Author
CEO and Founder of SanaView
janet@sanaview.com
©SanaView 2018. All rights reserved.

Chocolate Almond Balls/Truffles

This is another healthy alternative to cookies that are typically made with simple sugars and unhealthy fats. I was inspired to create this after visiting Brenda Davis, RD. She gave something similar to me as a treat for the flight back to Pittsburgh from British Columbia, Canada, and I absolutely loved them. Be careful because these are so good you will not be able to stop eating them!

Ingredients:

1 cup almond butter
1 cup of dates, soaked in water and drained
½ cup cocoa powder or raw cacao powder
Pinch of sea salt

Preparation:

If the dates are dry, soak them in a small bowl of water for a few minutes to moisten.
Drain the dates before using.
Otherwise, fresh dates work great as is.
Remove the pits and chop into small pieces.

Janet McKee Success Coach, Wellness Expert, Speaker and Author
CEO and Founder of SanaView
janet@sanaview.com
©SanaView 2018. All rights reserved.

Place all of the ingredients into a food processor and blend briefly to combine the ingredients.

Place 1 heaping tsp at a time into the palm of your hand and roll into a ball.
If the mixture does not stick together easily, add a bit of water or some additional dates.
Roll the balls in more cocoa powder to coat.

Servings: 12-24 balls depending on the size

Raw Chewy Chocolate Brownies

While teaching a class on the health benefits of chocolate with Adam Haritan, of Whole Foods Market, he inspired me to take my chocolate almond balls recipes and do a brownie variation using walnuts. It's basically the same recipe but by using raw walnuts instead of almond butter, you get more of a brownie consistency

Ingredients:
2 cups of raw walnuts
2 cups of dates, soaked in water to soften
1 cup cocoa powder or raw cacao powder
1 T vanilla
Pinch of sea salt

Preparation:
Place the walnuts in a food processor and grind them into a chunky walnut flower. Remove the dates from the water (saving some of the soaking water) and remove the date pits.
Place all of the ingredients into a food processor and blend briefly to combine the ingredients. Add some of the date soaking water if you need a bit more moisture to help the ingredients combine.
Press the mixture into a 9x9-baking dish and cut into squares and serve.

Servings: 16 small square brownies

Janet McKee Success Coach, Wellness Expert, Speaker and Author
CEO and Founder of SanaView
janet@sanaview.com
©SanaView 2018. All rights reserved.

Optional Raspberry Sauce:

Ingredients:
¾ C pitted dates, soaked in water and drained
1 T fresh lemon juice
1 ½ C frozen or fresh raspberries

Preparation:
Place all of the above ingredients in a blender and process into a sauce.

Sugar-Free Truffles
Adapted from a recipe by Dr. Anna Marie Clement of Hippocrates Health Institute

Ingredients:
¾ cup raw almond butter
½ cup sunflower seeds ground in a spice grinder
(you may soak and dehydrate before grinding if you have a dehydrator)
¼ cup raw sesame tahini
¼ cup hemp seeds
¼ cup of raw cacao or carob powder
1 ½ tsp ground cinnamon
½ tsp ground ginger
½ tsp ground nutmeg
2 T vanilla extract
15 - 20 drops of liquid stevia extract or to taste

Preparation:
Combine all of the ingredients in a mixing bowl or food processor, form into balls and roll in chopped nuts, or cacao powder, or shredded coconut or additional hemp seeds. Refrigerate and serve.

Servings: about 6 truffles

Vanilla Pudding
This is so simple and delicious and healthy that it is worth the effort of opening a young coconut!

Ingredients:
1 young "Thai" coconut
Vanilla extract
Vanilla bean

Preparation:
Opening a young coconut takes some practice and experience. Once you learn how to do it, it is relatively easy. First, slice the outside flesh off of the bottom until you find the natural hole in the hard shell. Poke at this hole until you are able to release the coconut water that is inside. Keep this water as you will need some for the recipe. The remaining water is wonderful to either drink straight for a refreshing beverage or save it for use in a smoothie.

Then, slice some of the soft outer white pith off the top to expose the hard shell. Hit the hard shell at an angle with a good strong knife or clever until the top pops off. This will give you access to the soft white meat inside which can be scooped out with a spoon.

Place the coconut meat, a bit of coconut water (to desired consistency), some vanilla extract and vanilla bean to taste in a blender and blend.

Servings: one individual serving per coconut

Optional Chocolate Pudding Variation
As if I haven't given you enough ideas on how to have chocolate creamy desserts, here is one more!!!

Add raw cacao powder to create chocolate pudding
You may need to add agave nectar if you desire a sweeter taste

Strawberry Parfait
Adapted from chef Juliano

Ingredients:
½ cup of pine nuts
1 cup water
½ cup of the meat from a young coconut
¼ cup honey (Optionally, try using less or no honey and using some of the young coconut water)
1 tsp salt (or less)
3 cups of frozen strawberries

Preparation:
Opening a young coconut takes some practice and experience. Once you learn how to do it, it is relatively easy. First, slice the outside flesh off of the bottom until you find the natural hole in the hard shell. Poke at this hole until you are able to release the coconut water that is inside. Keep this water and either drink it straight for a refreshing beverage or save it for use in a smoothie. You may try adding it to this recipe as a sweetener in place of the honey.

Then, slice some of the soft outer white pith off the top to expose the hard shell. Hit the hard shell at an angle with a good strong knife or clever until the top pops off. This will give you access to the soft white meat inside which can be scooped out with a spoon.

Blend all of the above ingredients and enjoy.

Servings: 4

Brazil Nut and Date Cookies
Adapted from Hippocrates Health Institute

Ingredients:
2 cups of Brazil nuts (optionally soaked & dehydrated for a truly raw version)
1 cup dates, pitted and soaked
2.5 T carob powder
1 T ground cinnamon

Preparation:
I simply combine all of the ingredients in a food processor until coarse "dough" is created.

Using a tablespoon of the mixture at a time, form into a ball or cookie shape of choice.

Servings: 12 cookies

Janet McKee Success Coach, Wellness Expert, Speaker and Author
CEO and Founder of SanaView
janet@sanaview.com
©SanaView 2018. All rights reserved.

Applesauce Oatmeal Cookies

From Your Organic Kitchen by Jesse Ziff Cool

Ingredients:
1 cup whole grain pastry flour
1 tsp baking powder
¾ tsp sea salt
½ tsp ground cinnamon
½ cup softened earth balance or coconut oil
1 cup of Organic Zero or Lakanto natural zero glycemic sweetener (or packed brown sugar)
1 vegan egg alternative
½ cup applesauce
¾ tsp vanilla extract
2 cups oats
½ cup raisins (optional)
¼ cup ground walnuts or pecans (optional)

Preparation:
Preheat oven to 375 degrees. Line a baking sheet with parchment paper.

In a medium bowl, combine flour, baking powder, salt and cinnamon. Set aside.

In a large bowl with an electric mixer on medium speed, beat the oil and sugar until light and fluffy. Add the egg replacement, applesauce, and vanilla extract.

Gradually combine the flour mixture with the wet mixture. Stir in the oats, raisins, and nuts.

Drop by large teaspoonfuls onto the prepared baking sheet. Bake the cookies for 10 minutes, or until lightly browned.

Servings: 36 cookies

Raw Chocolate Coconut Macaroon Cookies

This is a sweet treat but simple and great none-the –less.

Ingredients:
3 cups of dried, unsweetened coconut flakes
1 ½ cups of raw cacao powder
1 cup of maple syrup or agave nectar
1 T vanilla extract
Optional to add one Tablespoon of coconut oil
½ tsp salt

Preparation:
Combine all of the ingredients in a large bowl.

Using a large tablespoon, spoon rounds of cookie mixture onto a cookie sheet or dehydrator screen. Dehydrate at 115 degrees for 12 hours. If you don't have a dehydrator, put in the oven on the lowest possible temperature and check every so often and remove once they are slightly crisp on the outside and chewy on the inside.

Servings: 24 to 36 macaroons

Sweet and Healthy Coconut Balls
This is a healthier alternative to macaroons, as it does not use any simple sugar.

Ingredients:
3 cups of dried, unsweetened coconut flakes
¾ cups of chopped fresh dates
1 tsp vanilla extract
Pinch of sea salt

Preparation:
If the dates are dry, soak in a small bowl of water for a few minutes to moisten. Drain the dates before using.
Otherwise, fresh dates work great as is. Remove the pit and chop into small pieces.

Place 2 cups of the coconut flakes, vanilla and a pinch of sea salt into a food processor and blend briefly to combine the ingredients.

Add the chopped dates and blend until the ingredients begin to stick together.

Janet McKee Success Coach, Wellness Expert, Speaker and Author
CEO and Founder of SanaView
janet@sanaview.com
©SanaView 2018. All rights reserved.

Place 1 heaping tsp at a time into the palm of your hand and roll into a ball. If the mixture does not stick together easily, add a bit of water or some additional dates.

Roll the balls into the remaining coconut to coat.

Servings: 24 to 36 coconut balls

Cranberry Pecan Coconut Balls

This is an even more flavorful cookie/ball with the taste of cranberries and pecans.

Ingredients:
1/4 cup of dried, unsweetened coconut flakes
1/2 cup of chopped fresh dates
1 ½ cups pecans
1 cup dried cranberries (try to find the ones that are fruit juice sweetened)
½ cup almond butter
1 tsp vanilla extract
Pinch of sea salt

Preparation:
If the dates are dry, soak them in a small bowl of water for a few minutes to moisten. Drain the dates before using.
Otherwise, fresh dates work great as is. Remove the pit and chop into small pieces.

Place all of the ingredients except for the coconut flakes into a food processor and blend briefly to combine the ingredients until it creates a sticky dough.

Place 1 heaping tsp at a time into the palm of your hand and roll into a ball.
If the mixture does not stick together easily, add a bit of water or some additional dates.

Roll the balls into the coconut to coat.

Servings: 12-24 balls depending on the size

Raw Mango Pie

In a pinch one day, I needed to come up with a dessert to bring to a potluck gathering. Well, I took the ingredients I had on hand and inspiration from various raw food chefs and had fun creating what has become one of my favorite desserts. I keep this in the freezer for anytime my sweet tooth is kicking in.

Ingredients:
2 cups of almonds
½ cup of dates – soaked in water until soft
Pinch of sea salt
4 mangoes
4 bananas (optionally add slices from 2 additional bananas – see below)

Preparation:
Soak dates in water for 10 - 15 minutes until soft.
Remove dates from water and remove pits from the dates.

For the pie crust:
Place almonds in a food processor until it forms a course flour.
Add dates and a pinch of salt and process further.
Add some date soaking water if the crust is too dry.
Press the crust in a pie pan.

For the filling:
Add four mangoes and four bananas to the food processor and blend until smooth.
You may stir in slices from an additional two bananas if you choose.
Pour the mixture into the pie pan and freeze until firm before serving.

Servings: 8

Optional Fruit Pie Variation (Blueberry, Strawberry, Cherry or Peach Pie):
Use the same crust as above only change the filling as desired.

Ingredients for the filling:
5 or 6 cups fresh or frozen blueberries, strawberries, peaches, plums or cherries (thaw and drain well, if frozen)
3/4 cup pitted medjool dates, soaked
1 tablespoon fresh lemon juice

Preparation for the filling:
Place 1 1/2 cups of fruit along with the dates and lemon juice in a blender (you may also add an optional pinch of sea salt), and process until smooth.
Transfer to a mixing bowl, add the remaining fruit, and mix well.
Pour the fruit filling into the crust and spread with a rubber spatula.
This version of the pie does not need to be frozen.

Raw Apple Pie

This is the same recipe as the other berry and peach pies except I added cinnamon to give it more of an authentic apple pie flavor.

Ingredients:
Crust:
2 cups of almonds
½ cup of soaked dates with pits removed
Filling:
5 cups of thinly sliced apples
¾ cup of soaked dates with pits removed
1 T fresh lemon juice
1 tsp of ground cinnamon
For both, include a pinch of sea salt

Preparation:

For the crust, grind the almonds in a food processor until a chunky flour consistency is formed. Add the dates and a pinch of sea salt to the almonds and process further. Place the almond mixture in a pie pan or 9 x 12 pan and press evenly throughout to form the crust.

For the filling, blend 1 1/2 cups of sliced apples with ¾ cup of soaked dates, lemon juice, cinnamon and a pinch of sea salt in a blender to make the sauce. Pour the sauce over the remaining sliced apples and stir to coat evenly. Pour the apple mixture into the pie shell, sprinkle with more cinnamon, slice and serve.

Cut into thin slices or squares and serve with fresh berries.

Servings: 8

Raw Chocolate Pie

You may want to halve the recipe and use a thin tart pan instead of a pie pan for a chocolate tart as the pie filling is quite rich.

Ingredients:
For the Filling:
3 cups raw cocoa powder
2 cups agave nectar (optionally, try soaked fresh dates to avoid simple sugar)
1 cup lightly melted coconut oil
½ tsp sea salt

For the Crust:
2 cups almonds
½ cup dates, soaked and pitted

Preparation:
Grind the almonds in a food processor until a chunky flour consistency is formed. Add the dates to the almonds and process further. Place the almond mixture in a pie pan or 9 x 12 pan and press evenly throughout to form the crust.

Blend all of the ingredients for the filling in a food processor or blender until smooth. Pour the filling into the crust and chill for several hours before serving.

Cut into thin slices or squares and serve with fresh berries.

Servings: 16

INDEX:

Alfredo Sauce	Pg 122
Almond Milk	Pg 16
Almond Porridge	Pg 19
Apple Crisp – Low Sugar	Pg 157
Apple Pie – Raw	Pg 173
Apple Pie Smoothie	Pg 11
Applesauce Oatmeal Cookies	Pg 166
Asian Slaw	Pg 97
Asparagus Soup	Pg 49
Avocado Chocolate Mousse	Pg 155
Avocado – Creamy Dressing	Pg 88
Avocado Orange Dressing	Pg 85
Banana-Vanilla Pancakes	Pg 24
Basic Tahini Dressing	Pg 91
Berries with Cashew Whipped Cream	Pg 156
Berry Dessert Smoothie	Pg 151
Berry Smoothie	Pg 10
Black Bean and Corn Enchiladas	Pg 144
Black Bean Chili	Pg 81
Black Bean Dip	Pg 36
Blended Salad	Pg 101
Blue Sunset Smoothie	pg 10
Blueberry Banana Protein Smoothie	Pg 14
Blueberry Dressing – Oil Free	Pg 86
Blueberry Watermelon Freeze	Pg 12
Bok Choy – Ginger Over Rice	Pg 105
Brazil Nut and Date Cookies	Pg 165
Brazil Nut Milk	Pg 16
Brazil Nut Porridge	Pg 19
Breakfast	Pg 5
Broccoli Salad - Creamy	Pg 95
Broccoli Soup - Curried	Pg 68
Broccoli Soup – Farmer's Market	Pg 47
Broccoli – Steamed Winter Squash with Cauliflower	Pg 106
Broccoli – Tempeh Sauté	Pg 135
Brownies – Raw Chewy Chocolate	Pg 160

Janet McKee Success Coach, Wellness Expert, Speaker and Author
CEO and Founder of SanaView
janet@sanaview.com
©SanaView 2018. All rights reserved.

Brussels Sprouts with Ginger	Pg 112
Burger – Spicy Garbanzo	Pg 140
Butternut Squash and Red Pepper Soup/Ginger/Hemp Seeds	Pg 59
Butternut Squash Soup - Raw	Pg 60
Butternut Squash Soup with Fried Sage Leaves	Pg 57
Cantaloupe Smoothies	Pg 8
Carrot Ginger Soup	Pg 64
Cashew Milk	Pg 16
Cashew Whipped Cream	Pg 156
Cauliflower - Creamy	Pg 109
Cherry Chocolate Milk	Pg 148
Chewy Chocolate Brownies - Raw	Pg 160
Chickpea and Spinach Soup	Pg 65
Chili – Black Bean	Pg 81
Chocolate Almond Balls/Truffles	Pg 158
Chocolate Banana Frozen Dessert	Pg 154
Chocolate Banana Smoothie	Pg 10
Chocolate Brownies – Raw Chewy	Pg 160
Chocolate Cherry Acai Bowl	Pg 15
Chocolate – Mayan Hot Cocoa	Pg 146
Chocolate Mousse – Sugar Free Avocado	Pg 155
Chocolate Pie - Raw	Pg 175
Chocolate Pudding	Pg 163
Cleansing Smoothies	Pg 13
Coconut Balls	Pg 168
Coconut – Cranberry Pecan Balls	Pg 170
Coconut Curry – Janet's Vegetable	Pg 83
Collard Green Wraps - Raw	Pg 44
Cookies – Applesauce Oatmeal	Pg 166
Cookies – Brazil Nut and Date	Pg 165
Cookies – Raw Chocolate Coconut Macaroon	Pg 167
Cranberry Pecan Coconut Balls	Pg 170
Creamy Avocado Dressing	Pg 88
Creamy Broccoli Salad	Pg 95
Creamy Cauliflower	Pg 109
Creamy Cauliflower Potato Soup	Pg 51
Creamy Cucumber Dressing	Pg 88

Janet McKee Success Coach, Wellness Expert, Speaker and Author
CEO and Founder of SanaView
janet@sanaview.com
©SanaView 2018. All rights reserved.

Creamy Dressings	Pg 87
Creamy Miso Soup - Raw	Pg 54
Creamy Tahini Dressing	Pg 90
Creamy Zucchini Tahini Dressing	Pg 90
Curried Almonds - Raw	Pg 45
Curried Broccoli Soup	Pg 68
Curried Tofu Scramble with Spinach	Pg 23
Curried Zucchini Soup	Pg 69
Desserts - Truly Healthy and Decadent	Pg 145
Dressings - Salad	Pg 85
Dressing - Avocado Orange	Pg 85
Dressing - Basic Tahini	Pg 91
Dressing - Creamy Avocado	Pg 88
Dressing - Creamy Cucumber	Pg 88
Dressing - Creamy Tahini	Pg 90
Dressing - Creamy Zucchini Tahini	Pg 90
Dressing - French Alternative	Pg 85
Dressing - Fruity	Pg 86
Dressing - Honey Mustard	Pg 87
Dressing - Oil Free Blueberry	Pg 86
Dressing - Orange Tahini	Pg 91
Dressing - Pineapple Ginger	Pg 86
Dressing - Ranch	Pg 88
Dressing - Simple Lemon and Oil	Pg 85
Dressing - Simple Oil and Vinegar	Pg 85
Dressing - Simple Tahini	Pg 89
Dressing - Spicy Tahini	Pg 89
Enchiladas - Black Bean and Corn	Pg 144
Fall Harvest Pasta	Pg 126
Farmer's Market Fresh Broccoli Soup	Pg 47
French Dressing Alternative	Pg 85
Fresh Simple Salsa	Pg 33
Fruit Compote - Honey Vanilla	Pg 26
Fruit Pie - Optional Variation	Pg 172
Fruit - Simple Smoothie	Pg 7
Fruity Dressing	Pg 86
Garbanzo Burger - Spicy	Pg 140

Janet McKee Success Coach, Wellness Expert, Speaker and Author
CEO and Founder of SanaView
janet@sanaview.com
©SanaView 2018. All rights reserved.

Garlic Ginger Bok Choy Over Rice	Pg 105
Garlicky Greens	Pg 104
Granola – Raw Cranberry	Pg 27
Green Beans with Hazelnuts and Orange Zest	Pg 107
Green Smoothies	Pg 13
Greens with Pine Nuts and Raisins	Pg 102
Greens with Tahini Sauce	Pg 103
Guacamole	Pg 34
Health Snacks and Appetizers	Pg 29
Healthy Snack Ideas	Pg 30
Heart Warming Soups and Stews	Pg 46
Hearty Vegetable and Grain Soup	Pg 62
Hemp Protein Smoothie	Pg 12
Hemp Seed Milk	Pg 16
Honey Mustard Dressing	Pg 87
Honey-Vanilla Fruit Compote	Pg 26
Hot Cocoa – Mayan and Healthy Metabolism Raising	Pg 146
Hummus – Simple or Roasted Red Pepper	Pg 37
Hummus – Zucchini	Pg 39
Ice Cream	Pg 152
Janet's Asian Slaw	Pg 97
Janet's Mediterranean Rice Salad	Pg 131
Janet's Vegetable Coconut Curry	Pg 83
Janet's Yummy Rice	Pg 130
Juicing Suggestions	Pg 17
Kale and Collard Green Salad Raw - Italian	Pg 96
Kale Chips – Raw	Pg 42
Kale Chips – Spicy Raw	Pg 40
Kale Salad – Fresh Raw	Pg 93
Lemon and Oil Dressing	Pg 85
Lemony Smashed Potatoes	Pg 108
Lentil Artichoke Stew	Pg 76
Lentil Soup	Pg 56
Low Glycemic Smoothie	Pg 13
Low Sugar Apple Crisp	Pg 157
Macaroon – Raw Chocolate Coconut	Pg 167
Mango – Raw Pie	Pg 171

Janet McKee Success Coach, Wellness Expert, Speaker and Author
CEO and Founder of SanaView
janet@sanaview.com
©SanaView 2018. All rights reserved.

Mayan Hot Chocolate	Pg 146
Mediterranean Rice Salad – Janet's	Pg 131
Milk Shakes	Pg 149
Miso Soup	Pg 52
Miso Soup – Raw Creamy	Pg 54
Mousse – Sugar Free Chocolate Avocado	Pg 155
Nate's Favorite Breakfast Smoothie	Pg 11
Non-dairy Milk Smoothies	Pg 10
Nori Rolls – Raw	Pg 43
Nut Milk	Pg 148
Nut Milk Protein Smoothie	Pg 11
Nut or Seed Milk	Pg 16
Oatmeal Breakfast Porridge	Pg 20
Oatmeal Cookie - Applesauce	Pg 166
Oil and Vinegar Dressing - Simple	Pg 85
Oil Free Blueberry Dressing	Pg 86
Orange and Walnut Quinoa	Pg 129
Orange Tahini Dressing	Pg 91
Pancakes – Banana Vanilla	Pg 24
Pasta and Pasta Alternatives	Pg 113
Pasta – Fall Harvest	Pg 126
Pasta - Spring	Pg 117
Pasta with Butternut Squash, Sage and Greens	Pg 119
Pasta with Kale Tomatoes and Olives	Pg 118
Pasta with Simple Oil and Garlic	Pg 123
Pasta – Zucchini Raw	Pg 121
Peach Mango Smoothie	Pg 11
Pesto Sauce - Raw	Pg 122
Pie – Apple Raw	Pg 173
Pie – Optional Fruit Pie Variation	Pg 172
Pie – Raw Chocolate	Pg 175
Pie – Raw Mango	Pg 171
Pineapple Ginger Dressing	Pg 86
Porridge – Warm Grain	Pg 20
Potato and Winter Greens Soup	Pg 70
Potato Soup – Creamy Cauliflower	Pg 51
Potatoes – Lemony Smashed	Pg 108

Janet McKee Success Coach, Wellness Expert, Speaker and Author
CEO and Founder of SanaView
janet@sanaview.com
©SanaView 2018. All rights reserved.

Pudding – Chocolate and Vanilla	Pg 163
Quinoa and Vegetable Stew	Pg 77
Quinoa – Orange and Walnut	Pg 129
Quinoa Porridge	Pg 20
Ranch Dressing	Pg 88
Raspberry Sauce	Pg 161
Raw Alfredo Sauce	Pg 122
Raw and Dehydrated Soft Corn Tortillas	Pg 142
Raw Apple Pie	Pg 173
Raw (Blueberry, Strawberry, Cherry or Peach Pie) Variation	Pg 172
Raw Butternut Squash Soup	Pg 60
Raw Chewy Chocolate Brownies	Pg 160
Raw Chocolate Coconut Macaroon Cookies	Pg 167
Raw Chocolate Pie	Pg 175
Raw Collard Green Wraps	Pg 44
Raw Cranberry Granola	Pg 27
Raw Creamy Miso Soup	Pg 54
Raw Curried Almonds	Pg 45
Raw Fresh Kale Salad	Pg 93
Raw Italian Style Kale and Collard Greens Salad	Pg 96
Raw Kale Chips	Pg 42
Raw Mango Pie	Pg 171
Raw Nori Rolls	Pg 43
Raw Nut- Based Breakfast Porridge	Pg 19
Raw Pesto Sauce	Pg 122
Raw Seventh Heaven Soup	Pg 75
Raw Soup – Blended Salad	Pg 101
Raw Spicy Kale Chips	Pg 40
Raw Strawberry Parfait	Pg 164
Raw Tomato Sauce	Pg 122
Raw Walnut Tacos	Pg 138
Raw Wild Rice Cranberry and Pecan Salad	Pg 99
Raw Zucchini Pasta	Pg 121
Rice – Garlic Ginger Bok Choy	Pg 105
Rice – Janet's Mediterranean Salad	Pg 131
Rice – Janet's Yummy	Pg 130
Rice – Saffron with Pine Nuts and Asparagus	Pg 132

Janet McKee Success Coach, Wellness Expert, Speaker and Author
CEO and Founder of SanaView
janet@sanaview.com
©SanaView 2018. All rights reserved.

Risotto with Butternut Squash and Spinach	Pg 133
Roasted Red Pepper Hummus	Pg 37
Saffron Rice with Pine Nuts and Asparagus	Pg 132
Salad – Blended or Raw Soup	Pg 101
Salad Dressings	Pg 85
Salad – Creamy Broccoli	Pg 95
Salad – Janet's Asian Slaw	Pg 97
Salad – Janet's Mediterranean Rice	Pg 131
Salad – Spinach with Pears and Pecans	Pg 92
Salad – Raw (Fresh) Kale	Pg 93
Salad – Raw Italian Style Kale and Collard Green Salad	Pg 96
Salad – Wild Rice Cranberry and Pecan Salad	Pg 99
Salads and Side Dishes – Sumptuous	Pg 84
Salsa – Fresh Simple	Pg 33
Sautéed Asian Tempeh	Pg 136
Sautéed Veggies and Potatoes	Pg 21
Sesame Seed Milk	Pg 16
Seventh Heaven Soup	Pg 75
Side Dishes – Sumptuous Salads and Vegetable	Pg 84
Simple Freshly Cooked Tomato Sauce	Pg 124
Simple Fruit Smoothies	Pg 7
Simple Hummus	Pg 37
Simple Juicing Suggestions	Pg 17
Simple Lemon and Oil Dressing	Pg 85
Simple Oil and Vinegar Dressing	Pg 85
Simple Pasta with Oil and Garlic	Pg 123
Simple Spaghetti Squash	Pg 114
Simple Tahini Dressing	Pg 89
Simple Vegetable Noodle Soup	Pg 53
Simplest Ever Black Bean Chili	Pg 81
Slaw – Janet's Asian	Pg 97
Smoothie – Apple Pie	Pg 11
Smoothie – Berry	Pg 10
Smoothie – Blue Sunset	Pg 10
Smoothie – Blueberry Banana Protein	Pg 14
Smoothie – Blueberry Watermelon Freeze	Pg 12
Smoothie Bowls	Pg 15

Janet McKee Success Coach, Wellness Expert, Speaker and Author
CEO and Founder of SanaView
janet@sanaview.com
©SanaView 2018. All rights reserved.

Smoothie - Cantaloupe	Pg 8
Smoothie – Chocolate Banana	Pg 10
Smoothie - Cleansing	Pg 13
Smoothie - Green	Pg 13
Smoothie – Hemp Protein	Pg 12
Smoothie Inspiration	Pg 7
Smoothie – Low Glycemic	Pg 13
Smoothie – Nate's Favorite Breakfast	Pg 11
Smoothie – Non-dairy Milk	Pg 10
Smoothie – Nut Milk Protein	Pg 11
Smoothie – Peach Mango	Pg 11
Smoothie – Simple Fruit	Pg 7
Smoothie – Strawberry Peach Maca	Pg 14
Smoothie – Superfood	Pg 14
Smoothie – Tropical	Pg 12
Smoothie - Watermelon	Pg 8
Snack – Healthy Ideas	Pg 30
Soft Serve Ice Cream Frozen Dessert	Pg 152
Soups and Stews	Pg 46
Soup - Asparagus	Pg 49
Soup – Butternut Squash and Red Bell Pepper Ginger Hemp	Pg 59
Soup – Butternut Squash Raw	Pg 60
Soup – Butternut Squash with Fried Sage Leaves	Pg 57
Soup – Carrot Ginger	Pg 64
Soup – Chickpea and Spinach	Pg 65
Soup – Creamy Cauliflower Potato	Pg 51
Soup – Creamy Miso	Pg 54
Soup – Curried Broccoli	Pg 68
Soup – Curried Zucchini	Pg 69
Soup – Farmer's Market Broccoli	Pg 47
Soup – Hearty Vegetable and Grain	Pg 62
Soup - Lentil	Pg 56
Soup – Miso	Pg 52
Soup – Potato and Winter Greens	Pg 70
Soup – Raw Butternut Squash	Pg 60
Soup – Raw Creamy Miso	Pg 54
Soup – Raw Seventh Heaven	Pg 75

Janet McKee Success Coach, Wellness Expert, Speaker and Author
CEO and Founder of SanaView
janet@sanaview.com
©SanaView 2018. All rights reserved.

Soup – Simple Vegetable Noodle	Pg 53
Soup – Sweet and Spicy	Pg 74
Soup – Tomato Basil	Pg 72
Soup – Vegetarian Split Pea	Pg 66
Spaghetti Squash - Simple	Pg 114
Spaghetti Squash Primavera	Pg 116
Spicy Garbanzo Burgers	Pg 140
Spicy Raw Kale Chips	Pg 40
Spicy Tahini Dressing	Pg 89
Spinach Almond Dip	Pg 35
Spinach Salad with Pears and Pecans	Pg 92
Split Pea Soup – Vegetarian	Pg 66
Spring Pasta	Pg 117
Steamed Winter Squash with Broccoli and Cauliflower	Pg 106
Stew – Lentil Artichoke	Pg 76
Stew – Quinoa Vegetable	Pg 77
Stew – Vegetable with Spicy Sauce and Grains	Pg 79
Strawberry Parfait	Pg 164
Strawberry Peach Maca Smoothie	Pg 14
Sugar Free Chocolate Mousse	Pg 155
Sugar Free Truffles	Pg 162
Sumptuous Salads and Vegetable Side Dishes	Pg 84
Superfood Smoothies	Pg 14
Sweet and Healthy Coconut Balls	Pg 168
Sweet and Spicy Squash Soup	Pg 74
Sweet Potato or Yam Casserole	Pg 110
Tacos – Raw Walnut	Pg 138
Tacos - Tempeh	Pg 137
Tempeh Broccoli Sauté	Pg 135
Tempeh – Sautéed Asian	Pg 136
Tempeh Tacos	Pg 137
Tofu Scramble Ideas	Pg 22
Tomato Basil Soup	Pg 72
Tomato Sauce - Raw	Pg 122
Tomato Sauce – Simple Freshly Cooked	Pg 124
Tortillas – Raw and Dehydrated Soft Corn	Pg 142
Tropical Smoothie	Pg 12

Janet McKee Success Coach, Wellness Expert, Speaker and Author
CEO and Founder of SanaView
janet@sanaview.com
©SanaView 2018. All rights reserved.

Truffles – Chocolate Almond Balls	Pg 158
Truffles – Sugar Free	Pg 162
Truly Healthy and Decadent Desserts	Pg 145
Vanilla Pudding	Pg 163
Vegetable and Grain Soup	Pg 62
Vegetable Coconut Curry – Janet's	Pg 83
Vegetable Noodle Soup	Pg 53
Vegetable Side Dishes – Sumptuous Salads and	Pg 84
Vegetable Stew - Quinoa	Pg 77
Vegetable Stew with Spicy Sauce and Grains	Pg 79
Vegetarian Split Pea Soup	Pg 66
Veggie Burger - Garbanzo	Pg 140
Warm Grain Comforts and Hearty Main Dishes	Pg 128
Warm Grain Porridge	Pg 20
Watermelon Smoothies	Pg 8
Whipped Cream - Cashew	Pg 156
Wild Rice Cranberry and Pecan Salad	Pg 99
Winter Squash – Steamed with Broccoli and Cauliflower	Pg 106
Zucchini Hummus	Pg 39
Zucchini Pasta - Raw	Pg 121
Zucchini Soup - Curried	Pg 69

Janet McKee Success Coach, Wellness Expert, Speaker and Author
CEO and Founder of SanaView
janet@sanaview.com
©SanaView 2018. All rights reserved.

Made in the USA
Columbia, SC
22 June 2021